"*Crude Justice* is a page turner that reads like a crime novel—only the events documented in the book are all too real. In an era dominated by corporate PR and obfuscation, this book is a reminder of how difficult it is to shine a spotlight on even the most basic life-and-death stories from the frontlines of the energy economy. It is also a reminder of why those stories are so important and must be exposed."

—David Sirota,
author of the *New York Times* bestselling book *The Uprising*

CRUDE JUSTICE

CRUDE JUSTICE

HOW I FOUGHT BIG OIL AND WON,
AND WHAT YOU SHOULD KNOW
ABOUT THE NEW ENVIRONMENTAL
ATTACK ON AMERICA

STUART H. SMITH

BENBELLA

BENBELLA BOOKS, INC.
DALLAS, TEXAS

BenBella Books, Inc.
10300 N. Central Expressway
Suite #530
Dallas, TX 75231
www.benbellabooks.com
Send feedback to feedback@benbellabooks.com

Printed in the United States of America
10 9 8 7 6 5 4 3 2 1

Library of Congress Cataloging-in-Publication Data
   Smith, Stuart H., author.
   Crude justice : how I fought big oil and won, and what you should know about the new environmental attack on America / Stuart H. Smith.
      pages cm
   Includes bibliographical references and index.
   ISBN 978-1-939529-23-7 (hardback) — ISBN 978-1-940363-44-8 (electronic)
1. Liability for environmental damages—United States. 2. Petroleum industry and trade—Environmental aspects—United States. 3. Pollution—Law and legislation—United States. 4. Environmental protection—United States. 5. Environmental policy—United States. 6. BP Deepwater Horizon Explosion and Oil Spill, 2010. 7. Keystone XL Pipeline Project. 8. Fossil fuels—Environmental aspects—United States. I. Title.
   KF1298.S65 2015
   344.7304'6—dc23

                                                                    2014013736

Editing by Erin Kelley
Copyediting by Eric Wechter
Proofreading by Brittany Dowdle and Amy Zarkos
Indexing by Jay Kreider, Index It Now
Cover design by Faceout Studio, Emily Weigel
Author photo by Barry J. Cooper, Jr.
Text design and composition by John Reinhardt Book Design
Dust jacket printed by Brady Palmer
Printed by Lake Book Manufacturing

Distributed by Perseus Distribution
www.perseusdistribution.com

To place orders through Perseus Distribution:
Tel: (800) 343-4499
Fax: (800) 351-5073
E-mail: orderentry@perseusbooks.com

Significant discounts for bulk sales are available. Please contact Glenn Yeffeth at glenn@benbellabooks.com or (214) 750-3628.

To my best friend and partner, Barry J. Cooper, Jr.

CONTENTS

PROLOGUE: ROLLING THE DICE

A COMFORTABLE HOUSE on a suburban street, the big car parked out in front, children running around on freshly cut grass. If you've watched those slightly faded, blurry home movies from the mid-1960s, the glorious sepia-toned peak of the Baby Boom, then you have essentially seen my early childhood just outside of New Orleans.

In 1967, that idyll was permanently disrupted. It was a time of craziness all over the country, of riots in Newark and a Summer of Love in Haight-Ashbury—but I was a seven-year-old boy, too young to know about any of that. All I knew was that it was the year my life got turned upside down.

My father, Fredrick Smith, was at heart a decent man—a good father and an avid sportsman, albeit something of a risk taker. And then he was abruptly out of my life.

It would be years later when I pieced together what exactly had happened. A doctor told my dad that he had a severe congenital heart condition—and that he might not have long to live. My father apparently lost it at the news—and so he fled to a life filled with gambling and booze. It was when I was seven, the oldest of three boys, that my mom, Judy Smith, wanted no more of what she considered an aberrant lifestyle. She filed for divorce.

Throughout the rest of the '60s and '70s, Fredrick Smith, a playboy gambler, floated in and out of my life. He became a bookie and went on to open and operate casinos in private homes in Jefferson Parish, New Orleans. He lived hard and fast, trying to cram as much living as he could into his remaining years, while my mom did the hard work of raising a family.

Growing up in cramped apartments and then a modest home in New Orleans, watching my mom work two or three jobs to support us, was torture for me because I was just old enough to remember what we had lost. There was something burning inside of me, not just to get back to those suburban comforts, but to have more—to have so much that I wouldn't have to worry about losing it all in a single day.

My dad did leave me with something long before he left home— his attraction to risk. Fredrick Smith was a dice thrower, a wheel spinner, a stakes raiser...and so was I. Somehow I knew that I wasn't going to get where I wanted to go in this world playing one patient hand after another. No...I was determined to go for everything on one big toss.

BOOK
ONE

ONE

AN ATOMIC BOMBSHELL

T HE STORY OF MY LIFE is essentially split into two parts—everything that happened before April 14, 1986, and everything that happened after. The strange thing is that I didn't even realize the significance of that date until about three years after it had passed. Back on that spring morning, I was sitting in a classroom on the Loyola University law school campus in New Orleans.

Geographically, I hadn't gone very far in the world—I was still only a stone's throw from the string of Uptown apartments where my mom had struggled to raise me and two brothers while working multiple jobs. I was twenty-five, just days away from earning my law degree—and from jumping into an unsettled future. My ambitions upon graduation were bold but vague—to work in a big law firm where I could learn from the brightest lawyers and make a lot of money, which I needed to pay off my large student loan debt and

3

start working toward the life I wanted. I didn't know exactly how all that was going to play out.

I couldn't even begin to imagine that the events that would change everything were taking place 100 miles to the north of New Orleans, in a town called Laurel, Mississippi, on a small plot of land on a quiet rural road, heavily shaded by towering scrub pine. There stood an unremarkable prefab metal shed and a small side yard cluttered with piles of thick metal pipe from the nearby oil patch, shrouded in a heavy sheen of white dust.

The man who owned that two-acre plot was Winston Street, and on the morning of April 14, 1986, he was doing pretty much what he'd been doing every day since he'd ventured forth from the back-woods log cabin where he was raised: hustling to make a dollar. What had started out for Winston as a whim—an all-night project in a machine shop for a friendly customer—turned into his own thriving business once he finally found a bank that would lend him $500. Soon thereafter, he rigged up a machine that could clear out the gunk that piled up and clogged the miles of oil-production pipe that the big oil companies used inside their wells out in the Mississippi oil patch. So when the price of a barrel of crude shot up at the end of the 1970s, Winston had more work than he knew what to do with.

By 1986, world oil prices had plunged, but there was still plenty for Winston and his crew of a dozen men to do. Out behind the work shed, Winston's yard was stacked deep with pipe from every big oil company you could think of—Shell, Chevron, Mobil—waiting for a turn in his big machine that would bore out that pipe and send a cloud of white dust into the hot and humid air of Mississippi's lush green pine belt.

On this fateful day, a truck pulled onto the asphalt in the front of Winston's pipe-rattling yard. About three or four men got out, and the man in charge of these unannounced strangers introduced himself. He said his name was Eddie Fuente from the Mississippi Department of Health. Winston's first thought was that they were checking for spilled oil on his property, since hazardous waste and polluted groundwater had become a big issue in the 1980s. But Fuente explained that he was head of the state's Division of Radiological Health. Winston had not been aware that such an agency existed.

Fuente asked if his crew could take a look around the property, and that's when Winston saw the men unloading unusual equipment from the back of the truck.

The men carried Geiger counters.

"I knew what Geiger counters were from high school so I knew they were checking for radiation," Winston recalled later. Caught off guard, Winston allowed Fuente's men to walk up and down his yard with the metal boxes. "I just went back into the shop and let them do their thing."

The men with the Geiger counters spent around two hours walking around the property. When they were finally done, Fuente came back into the machine shop to talk with Winston.

"I didn't think anything of it right then," Winston said more than twenty-five years later, remembering the details as if it had happened only yesterday. "I didn't know what they was doing, but he come back after a couple of hours and talked to me and told me what the hell they was doing and told me what they had found." Fuente told him that if Winston had to send his men out to the yard, he should do it quick and make them come back inside immediately.

"What does that mean?" Winston asked Fuente. "Hell, I don't want them exposed to none of it if it's going to hurt them. I'm not going to send them out there at all."

"That probably would be the best thing to do," Fuente responded.

The significance of Fuente's words and the Geiger counters was starting to sink in for Winston. "That's what killed me right there," he later recalled.

He didn't understand all the science or all the specifics—that would come slowly, over the next five years—but the crux of what Fuente told him that morning was this: All the white scale dust that Winston and his machine had rattled out of miles and miles of oil-production pipes over the years—that silty mist that they breathed into their lungs every day, the thin white powder that caked their overalls every night—was laced with high levels of radioactive material, contamination that the oil companies pulled up from deep under the ground. It meant the end of Winston's thriving business—at best. At worst, the invisible radiation was going to make Winston and his workers very, very sick.

He knew he was going to have to clean up his property and get rid of all the radioactivity that had sent the needles spinning on Fuente's Geiger counters. And that was going to cost a lot of money—more than he had. He would have to convince his Big Oil clients to pay for it.

Or he was going to need a lawyer.

LEARNING TO QUESTION AUTHORITY

But back in April 1986, the odds that Winston Street would end up connecting with me were about as good as the odds of the then-hapless Saints making it to the Super Bowl. After all, I hadn't even finished law school yet, and it had been a tough road just to get to that point.

I didn't really have a very happy childhood. Part of the problem was money. I'd been born into the American dreamland of the early 1960s, a nice home in the upscale suburbs just west of New Orleans. But when my dad took up gambling and my parents split up when I was seven, everything changed overnight. My mother moved my two younger brothers and me back into the city, into a downstairs apartment in the Uptown neighborhood right near the Tulane and Loyola campuses.

It's not that we lived in abject poverty—Uptown was congested, but it was a leafy, comfortable urban neighborhood, home to lots of college students and the occasional record store or head shop. But everything became a struggle after my parents divorced, especially for my mother, Judy, who hailed from one of New Orleans's oldest families: the Toledanos. The family started out with a large land grant on the Mississippi Gulf Coast from the Spanish king and had been involved with founding the city's Cotton Exchange in the 1840s, before the Civil War, and then remained active in the high society of the boisterous city that perfected Mardi Gras. My maternal great-grandfather was a powerful local politician—the longest-serving president of the Jefferson Parish Police Jury, the equivalent of a county commission. My mother's dad was a successful insurance executive who moved into real-estate development—and got burned when an economic recession in the late 1950s hit New Orleans especially hard. My grandfather lost everything, so when my gambling-addled dad walked out on my mother, for her it was, as Yogi Berra is believed to have said, déjà vu all over again.

But whatever my mother lacked in resources, she made up for in resourcefulness. While my brothers and I were moved in and out of a series of Uptown apartments, she labored around the clock. She worked as a secretary, sold insurance and cosmetics, and eventually worked as a travel agent. She did whatever it took to pay the bills, and she worked like a dog. It wasn't until years later that my mom told me the reason we'd always stayed in our Uptown neighborhood: It was where she had attended high school in the Holy Name of Jesus Parish, and she kept up her connections there so that when she moved back, she convinced the parish to let us attend Catholic school tuition-free. She knew that education was the ladder up for her sons—I'm ashamed to admit that I didn't always hold up my end of the bargain.

Holy Name did save my brothers and me from some of the worst public schools in the country—but there was a price to pay. Although I excelled academically, I chafed at Catholic school discipline. Let's just say that the nuns at my school were not an easy bunch to get along with. I remember at one point I needed a haircut as dictated by the meanest nun in the school, Sister Marcello, but my mother didn't have the money to pay for it. Sister Marcello ended up dragging me over to the Loyola campus and paid the barber there to give me a haircut. I was mortified. Situations like that made me stronger and drove me on an almost mad quest toward absolute self-sufficiency.

Another one of Sister Marcello's common practices was to beat errant boys' hands with a giant pointer—a long wooden stick that was supposed to be directed at the words on the blackboard—that she always kept within arm's reach. She would drag you up to the front of the class and hold your hand and beat it with her trusty old stick, always saying with each whack, "O"-"B"-"E"-"Y." Is it any wonder that I grew up to become a legal advocate for the poor and working class against big corporations? My experiences at Holy Name deeply ingrained in me a distinct distaste for authority and the control the powerful have over the meek. Despite the discipline, Holy Name was a fantastic school. The financial assistance I received at Holy Name and at Loyola College of Law have a lot to do with my success. I always hoped that one day I would make it big and give something back to these Catholic institutions that had done so much for me.

I was a big kid who liked sports—especially the organized baseball games in the wide fields behind the city's home for wayward boys, a place my mom threatened to send me when I acted up or talked back, which was often. I rode my bike up and down the magnolia-lined streets, spending more and more time in the down-and-dirty record shops, searching the bins of LPs and indulging a passion for comic books.

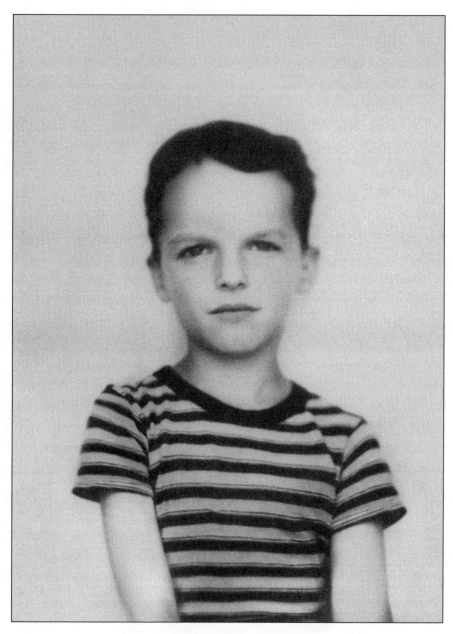

The author as a young boy.

Life got harder when I hit puberty. There were subtle things about me that were just different from the way the other boys acted sometimes—different ideas and mannerisms and youthful attractions, some of which I couldn't really put a name to, not yet anyway. From middle school on, other kids bullied me—usually it was verbal, but sometimes it was physical and occasionally quite brutal. I paid a heavy price for being different—even though it thickened my skin for things that would happen later on.

It probably didn't help that I was a bookworm, something of an egghead—eventually graduating from comic books to heavier literature, everything from Tolkien to Herman Hesse to Plato. I was a straight-A student in grade school but I got so bored by the time high school arrived that the drug culture—which was in its inglorious heyday in the mid-1970s—was too much of a temptation. I bounced through a couple of high schools and finally bounced out altogether in 1975. I was only fifteen—with no high school degree in a city suffering through yet another recession, its traditional manufacturing and shipping jobs vanishing into the haze of the brutally hot Louisiana Bayou.

The funny thing is that despite my less-than-stellar academic career so far, I still had this idea in the back of my head that I might have a career in law. I had never forgotten my first real argument. It was with my beloved grandfather, Joe Montaldo, when I was still in school. We were having a heated discussion about who the best musicians were in the world at the time. This was about 1969 or 1970—just as the hippie counterculture was peaking. I put forth my best argument for the Beatles, their rich body of work and the genius of both McCartney and Lennon on full display, as well as the more mortal talents of Ringo and George. My grandfather emphatically embraced Elvis Presley, and with good reason—he was the King. My grandfather never conceded but did say, in the end, with a sigh and a shake of his head, "You argue too much. You should be a lawyer when you grow up."

Now, as I was no longer in school, my parents ordered me to go to work. I stocked supermarket shelves for a while, until I found out that I had a knack for the art of telephone solicitation. I sold magazine subscriptions at first, and then I was offered a job selling bars to keep out burglars—cold-calling residents of various New Orleans neighborhoods. In the mid-to-late 1970s, fears about crime were running amok in the Crescent City. I sold a lot of burglar bars.

But that kind of hustle also made me realize that I really belonged back in school. The final motivator was watching my first cousin Jennifer start her freshman year at Louisiana State University in Baton Rouge. A short time later I earned my GED, and I enrolled in LSU that January, only a few months behind my former classmates. Like a lot of working-class students in the late 1970s, I was helped by low in-state tuition. I studied philosophy by day and kept on hustling at night, selling magazine subscriptions and helping my mom with some travel agency work. It was the time of the Islamic revolution in Iran, and there was a large group of Iranian students in Baton Rouge, some of whom enlisted me for help in finding a route that would get them back to Tehran in the summer of 1981. I'm still haunted to this day by what happened to them: The majority were conscripted into the Iranian Army to fight Iraq's Saddam Hussein and his poison gas. Many of them never made it back to Louisiana to finish school.

Ironically, I had protested on campus against the deposed Shah as I was somewhat politically active during my college years. I'd been a Democrat since I was twelve, kind of by accident at first. In 1972, a teacher was dividing up our class for a mock presidential debate. In our neighborhood, a white conservative bastion of New Orleans, all the kids wanted to be the incumbent Richard Nixon—myself included! But out of all the other kids, the teacher assigned me to argue for McGovern, so after school while throwing my paper route in the dormitories on Tulane's campus I wandered a couple of blocks over to the Tulane student union building, where antiwar students had tables, passing out literature for the upstart Democrat. They convinced me that it was McGovern looking out for the working people—and I've never looked back since.

But I'd be lying to you if I told you that politics, or some kind of sense of social justice, was the main thing that was driving me as a young man. The circumstances of my upbringing—starting out in suburban comfort and falling abruptly into the struggles of the working poor—were my guiding light. I realize this might sound crass to some, but I think I was more driven to succeed and make a lot of money. I grew up with people who had a lot of money—and I wanted to have more than them. When my father died when I was twenty-one—the congenital heart problem that had triggered his gambling spree finally took his life while he was on the waiting list for a transplant—my sorrow only seemed to heighten my resolve to go very far in a short period of time.

The law career that my grandfather predicted for me seemed exactly the right path—a good fit for both my talent in the art of arguing and my oversized career ambitions. By 1983, I was back home in Uptown New Orleans as an incoming law student at Loyola University College of Law. In hindsight, all the elements that made me the attorney that I am today—hardworking, uncompromising, competitive, risk-taking, and a champion of the underdog against the unbridled authority of the powerful—were all simmering at that young age. But it still took a couple of events to bring everything into focus.

The first was another family tragedy. This time it was the death of my younger brother Whitney.

My brother's death was one of those completely senseless and inexplicable episodes of the human existence that just crushes you. He was hit by a car while crossing a road in Destin, Florida. Just like that. Whitney hadn't yet turned twenty-one. He suffered a catastrophic head injury and was declared brain-dead by doctors at

Stuart during his law-school days.

the hospital. He was on life support for several days while we went through the agonizing process of figuring out what to do next. My mother had to make the final decision to have him removed from life support and donate his organs. It was her call and making it, as you might imagine, left a deep scar on her entire being and a lasting impression on me and my brother Clark.

Whitney's death brought about my first direct experience with a court case. My brother had been killed because he had walked across an area where workers were doing road construction earlier in the day, a zone through which no cars were permitted to drive. He was standing there waiting to cross, and a car came careening right through the no-traffic zone and ran him down. It was a case of what is benignly called "improper channelization of traffic."

I found out about the accident at a moot court competition in Houston and rushed to the scene. It changed me, watching my mother cry uncontrollably for days at the hospital and for days until the funeral. The grief was right on the surface of our lives for the next several years, and sadness permeated our home. My mother would burst out crying for no apparent reason, repeatedly on the bad days.

To make a tragic situation even worse, one of the attendants fumbled while trying to get Whitney into the ambulance. They dropped the gurney and my brother fell on his already-injured head. I set about researching the case and finding a suitable attorney to represent us.

The most insulting and demoralizing part of the situation was the legal process—my mother's deposition in particular. The defense lawyer treated her terribly, speaking down to her like she wanted something for nothing. I bit my tongue raw that day, struggling not to yell at the lawyer who was doing his best to make my mother feel small. All I knew was that the defendant had dropped my injured brother on his head while trying to get him in the ambulance. My mother trembled and cried continuously through her entire deposition— an image I haven't been able to shake for more than twenty years. I felt helpless witnessing my mother's anguish, unable to do a damn thing about it. I haven't cried since that day, except at my grandmother's funeral. But I knew as soon as that smug defense attorney deposed my mother that I wanted to hold people accountable for hurting others.

Maybe that's why I found my first job out of law school so unsatisfying. It was in a big legal defense firm—a silk-stocking kind of place, very stodgy. My first cases were what they called maritime defense—mostly defending against longshoremen who were injured on the job in Louisiana's shipping industry, still a major employer at that time. It was a little like the legal equivalent of working as a resident after medical school.

But defense was simply not in my genes. I found working for the large companies that owned ships more than a little unfulfilling— probably because my gambler's DNA craved risk and the chance of

Stuart with his mother on the day he graduated law school.

a huge payday, the kind of thrill that only came from practicing tort law on the side of the plaintiff. I wanted to fight big corporations, not do their bidding. I was chomping at the bit, looking around for adventure and the sense that there was more to life than taking on blue-collar workers who'd slipped on a desk somewhere. However, I will be forever grateful to those lawyers who gave me a chance and taught me so much.

After a year and a half, though, I jumped at the chance to work with a real New Orleans character, a trial lawyer named Jack Harang. He was a sharp dresser and had an equally sharp mind inside the courtroom, but he had little patience for the kind of behind-the-scenes hard work that it often takes to win a case. He was habitually late for everything. The only thing that he managed worse than the clock was his checkbook. And I'll never forget the day on one of our early cases together when I dragged Jack to the law library to look

Stuart with Jack Harang at Mardi Gras.

something up. He protested as we entered, "I haven't been in a law library in twenty years!"

But Jack was savvy about the law and a brilliant trial lawyer. He specialized in maritime accidents and accidents at offshore oil rigs—representing workers, not the corporations—and I can honestly say that those industries got a lot safer in Louisiana because of the aggressive work that he and others like him did. Around this time, Jack was becoming a pioneering lawyer in pursuing nursing home abuse cases. I learned quite a bit from Jack—even as I looked to carve out my own niche. He taught me his creed for the brutal work of a trial lawyer. "You eat what you kill," he told me. "If you don't kill, you don't eat."

The decade of the 1980s brought a new focus on the field of environmental law; in the wake of scandals like Love Canal, Three Mile Island, *Exxon Valdez*, and Times Beach there was suddenly a greater public awareness about hazardous wastes and other kinds of chemical pollution, and the Deep South had more than its share of illegal dumping. That said, there was nothing particularly remarkable about my first few cases.

Until one day in 1989 when the telephone rang.

On the other end of the line was Winston Street. And things were never going to be the same for me.

"SCARING EVERYBODY TO DEATH"

Winston Street was born in a two-room log house about thirty miles east of Laurel, Mississippi, in a rugged, independent county they still call "the Free State of Jones." His house didn't have locks on the doors—just a chintzy wooden latch. No one locked their doors in that neck of the woods back then anyway, and when it got hot—which was often in southern Mississippi—the family would just sleep out in the front yard, under the stars. Winston's daddy started out farming the land just like his ancestors, and sometimes he'd cut down trees and sell wooden ties to the railroad. "He got a nickel apiece," Winston told me. "It would take me two weeks to cut a twelve-by-twelve crosstie— but he could do five or six a day." His early life reads like a lost chapter out of Walker Evans and James Agee. Everyone picked cotton at harvest time. When someone from nearby killed a pig, there was usually a big pig roast, and folks saved a little money by making their own soap by forming lye from the bark of red oak trees and mixing it with lard. It wasn't all work. As a young man, Winston also learned that uniquely Southern art—the steel guitar—and he remains one of the top players in south-central Mississippi to this day, venturing out to churches with a local country combo.

But change was starting to come to Mississippi in the middle of the twentieth century—economic change. Industry started moving down to the Deep South in search of cheaper labor costs, and thanks to the state's long-serving and powerful Democratic lawmakers, the Gulf Coast was now a hub for shipbuilding and other military contracting. But nothing would change Winston's life more than the region's oil boom. When he was growing up, his dad took a job working in the oil patch, and Winston took his first summer job in the nearby oil fields when he was only seventeen. After high school, he found work in the local machine shops where the oil drillers were his best and most frequent customers.

"I tell you what got me into business," he said. "A businessman came into the shop I was working in and needed a piece made, and he'd been to all the machine shops in town trying to get somebody to make that piece. He worked with Baker Oil. It was a bad job—I worked on it all night. The end had to be three inches inside that piece with a step thread—I got that made for him and there was another guy that I made stuff for and both of them come to me one day and said, 'Look, if you go into business for yourself we'll give you all the work we can.'"

By the 1970s, Winston's skill at machining different types of pipes and heavy equipment that the big companies needed in the Mississippi oil patch took him all over the country; at home he kept hiring more and more folks as all the big players in the industry— Halliburton, Exxon, Chevron, and Shell—brought him new types of work. This was the era of gas station lines and Arab oil embargoes, when the price of a barrel of crude shot to unimaginable highs and the major players sunk those windfall profits into oil exploration here at home. By the turn of the decade, the machine shop that eventually became known as simply Street, Inc. had enough work for forty-five people, including Winston's younger brother Clark.

It was around that time that Winston made a life-altering decision.

"There was an ol' boy that came to me one day and he had an idea for building a pipe-cleaning machine—one that would clean out the inside of the oil-field tubing, and he built the machine and he never could make it work," as Winston recalls it. "Since I kind of had a hand in working with it, he came to me one day and offered to sell it, and I paid him $12,000 for the machine and a one-ton truck that it went on. It was a crude thing the way he had it set up—it took two hours to drill through a piece of tubing—and when I got through with it you could drill through it in about three minutes."

That meant a lot of new business for Street, Inc. because oil and gas production brings up ancient seawater brine along with the oil and gas. A lot of this comes up as what the oil companies call "produced water," and back in the 1980s most of this toxic wastewater was still getting dumped in unlined pits in some of America's poorest communities. But solids in the briny matter condensed out and coated the inner walls of the production pipe. In the industry, they call this material "scale," and if it accumulates long enough, it starts to gunk up the pipes to the point where it restricts the flow of oil, increasing the time and the cost of producing a barrel of crude. That's when they'd call a contractor like Street, Inc., who had the machinery for blasting that scale out of the inside of the pipe. It turned out that Winston was one of only two contractors in the state of Mississippi who could do this highly specialized work. They called it pipe rattling or reaming. With the oil boom peaking in the early 1980s, the trucks from the big oil giants were practically lined up outside his little two-acre yard—he even stored a lot of pipe on another eight-acre tract that he owned. Every time that Winston's $12,000 contraption did its job, the white briny dust went flying all over the place, eventually coating his shop and every inch of ground like a gentle snowstorm. A lot of Winston's work was also in the oil field because he could mobilize the equipment and clean the pipe at the wellhead.

By 1986, the worldwide price of crude had collapsed, and American oil and gas production went from boom to bust practically overnight. Winston had to let a lot of his workers go, and by the spring of that year he was down to only a dozen or so employees, including his brother Clark. Thanks to his pipe cleaning machinery, Winston's operation was still a highly profitable one. Indeed, shortly before the tumultuous events of 1986, he'd had his best month ever, bringing in $280,000. Then, around March, something very strange happened at the shop.

A couple of men representing one of his biggest customers, the oil giant Chevron, stopped by the shop. One of them introduced himself as H.T. Miller. That name meant nothing to Winston; later he would learn that Miller was a prominent health physicist, which is a highly specialized job that analyzes radiation risk and protection—how radiation affects people and the surrounding environment, and how best to minimize adverse health effects.

On this fine Mississippi spring day, the men from Chevron muttered something about looking for ways to reduce levels of radiation, but they did so in such a way that it didn't really occur to Winston or his crew that there was any significant risk at hand. It sounded more like environmental talk than something that was immediately affecting the health of his men. The visitors spent a lot of time looking over Winston's drill-out machine, the device he'd created to rattle the oil pipes. "And one of them asks me if there was any way that I could fix it so none of the shavings or drilled-out scale got on the ground. And I told them, 'yeah, I can do that, but it would be expensive to rig it up like that.' And he said, 'Well, there is some stuff come up, that we can't let any of it get on the ground anymore.'"

Winston never got the chance to re-rig the machine. He didn't have the time or the money, and the Chevron men hadn't made it sound that important. It was only a couple of weeks later when Eddie Fuente and his team of Mississippi inspectors showed up at the shop with their Geiger counters. He told Winston that the team had found radiation on his site at thousands of times above normal background levels, far exceeding the allowable exposure level for workers. The state regulator also explained that Chevron had recently discovered high levels of radiation at its Raleigh oil field in central Mississippi, triggering a search by regulators across the region to find the extent of the problem. Fuente told Winston that he would have to get a special radioactive materials license to continue cleaning the pipes and that the material could not get on the ground.

Before that day no one had ever told Winston that the briny scale on the inside of those pipes was radioactive. The inconvenient truth for the oil industry is that the saltwater contains radioactive material— mainly radium-226 and radium-228—that exists naturally, all around us, mostly in small amounts. There are trace amounts of radium in soil and rock, for example, but the quantities are so small that they pose little health risk except when radon, a dangerous gas that can cause cancer, occasionally seeps into the basement of homes. However, naturally occurring radium goes from relatively harmless to downright deadly when it becomes as highly concentrated as the scale on the inside of oil-field piping or when it's dumped into open pits as brine-filled wastewater.

Winston hardly knew what to make of all of this new information. When the first group from Chevron came out, he didn't think there was anything to worry about. But after his encounter with Fuente, he panicked. Not only did he shut down his operation to keep the workers from any new exposure to the dust that he now realized could be deadly, but also he put up large signs to keep his neighbors off the property. Soon, the townsfolk of Laurel, Mississippi, were just as upset as Winston.

"The word got around about it," Winston recalled, ruefully. "We had some kids on go-carts. They'd come out and turn around on my land, the storage area and loading dock. I didn't care as long as they didn't get on my pipe racks. When I thought about it, I roped it off and put a sign out that said KEEP OFF—RADIOACTIVE! Well, I didn't want them exposed to more of that stuff than they had to be. Boy, people started coming by and looking, and all that stuff." A neighbor across the road even blamed Winston for a watermelon that kind of looked like it had three heads.

"They said I was trying to scare everybody to death," he said.

One way or the other, Winston knew he needed the property cleaned up as soon as possible. Early in the crisis, a specialist from the U.S. Environmental Protection Agency (EPA), at Fuente's request, visited Winston and told him the hard truth that it could cost him as much as $2 million to clean up the property fully. And since Winston didn't have $2 million, the government man told him, he would probably have to sue somebody.

Winston summoned two officials from Chevron to come out and meet him. "I told them I don't want to sue. If you come out and clean it up, I'll sign whatever to release your liability. I want to get back to work." According to Winston, one of the men from Chevron said, "we're not going to clean it up. We'll advise you on what you need to do to clean it up."

That just didn't cut it. So he sued. Eventually, some thirty-four of the men who had worked at Winston's pipe-rattling yard and their family members signed on to the lawsuit against two of his major, deep-pocketed Big Oil customers, Shell and Chevron.

But justice would not be easy. For one thing, Winston quickly learned that suing two such powerful companies meant that he was all but blackballed from any future oil-patch work, except for one loyal customer from Halliburton who still came by with the occasional job. An equally daunting problem was that winning a case against Shell and Chevron would mean finding an attorney who was willing to take on Big Oil's high-priced legal guns, and who had the knowledge and gumption to beat them in a courtroom if it came to that. In the backwaters of south-central Mississippi, that was easier said than done.

The first lawyer who Winston hired was a well-known Mississippi attorney named Stanford Young. Young, who was in his early seventies, was a real character. One of his trademarks was that he always wore all black and drove a big black Cadillac, a grim reminder of the tragic day that he ran over his own son in a freak accident. He also had a way with words. Touring the Street property with a crew with Geiger counters, Young joked that "every click is another $5!" But as he managed the Street case, it seemed to the plaintiffs that Young was more interested in a quick, down-and-dirty settlement with the oil giants than in long-term litigation in court that is often required to achieve the type of justice that they were interested in.

One day not long after Winston and his employees filed their federal lawsuit, there was a status hearing on the case before a judge in Hattiesburg. It was supposed to be routine. In fact, Winston didn't even go—thanks to the blackballing of his own yard, he'd taken a job at another machine shop to make ends meet. But his brother Clark—who'd been working at the machine shop before the men with the Geiger counters showed up and now had thrown himself full-throttle into every aspect of the case—drove down there.

In the middle of the day, Winston got a surprise phone call from his younger brother.

"Well, Winston, we done gone as far with it as we can go," Clark told his startled brother. "Stanford settled it!"

Winston found out that Chevron would have paid about $200,000 under the tentative deal that Young had agreed to. Not only was that grossly inadequate to compensate him and his workers for the loss of the business, the health risks, and any cleanup of the site, but it also ignored the fact that Winston and Clark were in the process of developing powerful evidence that the oil giant had knowingly sent radioactive pipe to the yard in Laurel. So $200,000 just wasn't good enough. It wasn't even close.

"I can't get any more blood out of this turnip," Young tried to explain when a furious Winston met with him in his office. Seeing the angry look on his client's face, Young then insisted that now that he understood what Winston wanted, he swore he would come up with a strategy for winning the case at trial. It was too late. Winston fired him on the spot.

Unfortunately this was the start of a trend.

The list of qualified attorneys who would take on clients like the Streets was a pretty short one, and the roster of lawyers who'd actually bring their case to trial was even shorter. In the legal profession, we call a case like this one a "black hole." Chevron and Shell had deep pockets and the top defense lawyers on their team. Taking them on before a judge and jury would require years of research, with cross-country travel and lining up of medical and scientific experts. But Streets's attorneys wouldn't get one thin dime to pay for any of that without a settlement or a jury verdict down the road. This is a central concept of the film *A Civil Action*, where the cash-poor tort lawyers rifle through about thirty credit cards to find one to pay a hotel bill. Only a fool or a gambler would take this on. After hiring and firing three different sets of lawyers, Winston started asking around for recommendations. One Mississippi lawyer said that while he didn't want to touch the case, he would give him the name of a promising lawyer who was suing his client up in Jackson, Mississippi, over alleged pollution by a tire company. That young attorney was me.

At this point, the fact that I was only twenty-nine, with little more than a year of environmental law under my belt, and had been barely out of law school when the Street case began, didn't matter all that much. Heck, all that was probably a plus.

Winston picked up the phone and made that call, asking me to come to Laurel and talk with him about taking the case.

I certainly had to think about it. There were good reasons that so many other lawyers had passed on the case—or been fired by Winston. I knew this case would have a much higher profile in the media and in the legal community than anything I had done before; meaning that if I lost, I could do enormous damage to my reputation before my career had really started rolling. What's more, the Street case would in all probability set a precedent for future claims against the oil industry for radioactive contamination. There would be enormous pressure on Big Oil to win, and win at any cost. I talked to friends, family, and colleagues—and many of them advised me not to take the case.

I called Winston back and told him I was coming up right away, with our law firm's investigator, Ron Hirsch. Something inside me was telling me I had to roll the dice on this one.

But there was one more thing about Winston and me hitching our fortunes together. I knew from the first time that I heard his thick-as-molasses backwoods accent that we would be quite the odd couple. I had grown up in an urbane bookish world of the mind, bracketed by two of the South's great universities, while Winston's childhood experience had been defined by hunger and hard manual work. I was a McGovern Democrat and Winston was a Reagan Republican. When he was in country roadhouses wailing on the steel guitar, I was likely in a nightclub listening to the New Wave music of the B-52s or Joy Division. And the things that we did have in common—our feistiness and distrust of authority, whether it was pointer-wielding nuns or know-it-all lawyers—only meant that there would surely be times we would be at each other's throats. Especially in that rebellious, independent place they called the Free State of Jones.

And then there was one more thing...remember the bullying I'd experienced in school, the attractions that I kept to myself? By the time I was twenty-nine, I had long decided to live as an openly gay man, even in such a conservative time as the Reagan years and in such a conservative place as the Deep South. That had not been a major problem in New Orleans, the Southern outpost of *bon temps rouler*—but how would it play in the thick woods of Mississippi, with the Street brothers and a largely rural jury pool? Frankly, I had no idea.

In spite of our surface differences, I could feel that Winston and I were kindred spirits. We'd both grown up feeling deprived, motivated by a burning desire to better ourselves at any cost, and to fight anyone who stood in our way. I had a hunch that we were going to work together just fine.

"I'm going to be honest, it wasn't because I thought he'd be good," Winston admitted years later, talking about hiring me. "I'd run out of options. The judge was so mad at me he was about to run me out the courtroom."

In 1989, more than three years had passed since the day that the men with the Geiger counters had shown up at Winston's front door. Hiring and firing lawyers wasn't the only thing that Winston and his brother Clark had been up to during all that time. When Jack and I finally sat down to meet them, it was as if the Street brothers had been running a kind of radiological detective agency on the side. And they had a remarkable story to tell.

TWO

THE CURIOUS CASE OF
THE PAINTED SPIDER

IT WAS JUST A FEW DAYS after the phone call from Winston Street that I found myself in Laurel, sitting at the kitchen table of Winston's comfortable split-level home, nestled against the edge of the southern Mississippi pine belt, back along an old country road. That morning I'd climbed into my convertible with Ron Hirsch and made the two-and-a-half-hour drive up to Laurel—still wondering if this was a giant waste of time, taking this "black hole" of a case that had already driven away so many lawyers.

Our mission that morning was to check out the pipe shop and get the lay of the land, but mainly we just wanted to eyeball Winston Street and his brother Clark, in order to get a sense of who they were and what kind of witnesses they might be if this case ever went to

trial, and to get more details on the case against Chevron. I knew that
Jack Harang back in New Orleans was eager for a positive report,
because with the slowdown in oil drilling and maritime cases, he
was looking for new avenues of litigation to bring in some money.
Of course, after everything they'd been through with the legal profession, the Streets still harbored reasonable doubt about us as well.

Winston had a soft doughy face and spoke in a deep, thick
Southern backcountry accent, as thick and acidic as a jug of Coca-
Cola syrup undiluted by soda water. He peppered his tale of radioactive woe with rural colloquialisms and barnyard language. Clark
was a very different cat—bearded, wiry, less outgoing, a little more
sophisticated, and a lot more direct.

The Street brothers were wizards with industrial machinery, but
they'd had little book learning since high school, a couple of decades
earlier. But now, with the radioactive contamination closing down
their shop, the two brothers threw all of their energy and most of
their spare time into their case, which consisted of learning the basics
of nuclear science. Winston and Clark apparently figured that if they
could stay up all night and design a machine to clean the scale out of
oil pipe, there was no reason they couldn't learn how to unravel the
secrets behind radioactive scale.

As I listened to their story, I realized that in the three years since
Eddie Fuente had shown up at their shop with a Geiger counter, the
Street brothers had become a pair of southern-fried radiation detec-
tives. Bitter and dismayed over what had happened to their pipe-
cleaning business, they became fixated on proving their suspicion
that the Big Oil companies had known that their pipes were chock-
full of radiation well before 1986. Since their first batch of lawyers
had proved incompetent, indifferent, or both, they figured that they'd
just go out and build the case themselves.

In those early, nerve-wracking days—their padlocked-shut,
radium-laced property in Laurel making them pariahs back

home—Winston and Clark wanted to start by establishing the chain of evidence—to find out for themselves where this radioactive dust that had turned their lives upside down was coming from. So they talked their first attorneys into finding them a Geiger counter, and they bought a rudimentary video camera. In the name of discovery in their lawsuit, they decided to call on their ex-customers in the Mississippi oil patch by going to the well locations from which pipe had been removed and cleaned by Street, Inc.

Shell and Chevron had been the Streets' two largest customers; they were the obvious places to start. For the oil companies, their first and simplest line of defense would be to claim there was no way of proving that they were the source of the radioactive scale that ended up in the Street pipe yard. After all, their machine shop serviced a lot of different customers over the years. To counter that, Winston and Clark wanted to go out to the companies' oil fields, to show that their wells were already laced with radioactivity before they were cleaned at the well location or loaded on trucks and brought to Laurel. The oil companies did not count on the fact that Winston kept meticulous financial records that identified all the cleaning jobs and which well they were associated with.

By then, of course, they had already retained their initial lawyers and filed suit; under the rules of evidence, any site visit would now be considered part of the discovery process and would have to be negotiated in advance. That robbed the Street brothers of the crucial element of surprise, but they still thought it would be hard for the oil companies to completely hide the evidence, after decades, they suspected, of pulling so much radium up from the ground.

One of the first site visits they'd arranged was at Shell's facility at Tallahala Creek, about twenty miles north of Laurel. The oil was delivered to this facility from the wellheads to be processed, meaning that this was the place where the salty, radium-laced water was separated from the crude oil. The scale-lined pipes that pumped the mixtures were serviced and stored inside a large warehouse near the creek. The Streets' records showed that they had both cleaned pipe from this oil field at their shop and also at the well site. The goal was to find evidence of contamination associated with the oil production in the field. If established, the Streets could rightly prove that all of the pipe cleaned from this field was also, more probably than not, hot.

Shell had been one of their biggest customers, but now—as they related to me and Ron over their kitchen table—when they showed up at the front gate with a Geiger counter that their then-attorney had loaned them, it looked different from their earlier visits. Indeed, it looked like no industrial site the men had ever seen before. Everything was lined up on shelves in perfect order—like the shoe closet of an obsessive-compulsive man. The floor of the main warehouse was so clean that you could eat off it, Winston told us. And they were getting nothing at all on the Geiger counter. Looking around, the brothers could not find so much as a cigarette butt on the ground. It didn't make sense; surely the radioactive pipe must have passed through this Shell facility on its way to the Streets' cleaning yard.

Discouraged, they decided to also check some of the wells in the field from which they had cleaned pipe. They were also spotless and clean as a whistle. Just as they were getting ready to leave, one of the brothers saw something bizarre. There was a flange on the well-head assembly that was freshly painted over, obviously in a hurry, since the spider's web that was directly behind it was also painted. A black spider crawled out from behind the flange—and its back, too, was covered in a fresh coat of yellow paint, the color of a Shell gas station sign. Everything looked so clean in the field because, they believed, it had been frantically cleaned up and painted in the hours before the Street brothers arrived, probably in the hope of deadening any lingering radioactive particles. But they reasoned that if a hastily executed cover-up had taken place, then the radioactive material should still be close by.

With the Geiger counters in tow, they turned around and began surveying the facility in concentric circles at greater and greater distances, expanding their search now to cover the grounds away from the well. Suddenly, at the far end of the worksite, the Geiger counters started crackling and the needles jumped. The Street brothers kept walking off the Shell property, away from the company's wells and its storage facility, and found themselves in the middle of a farmer's watermelon patch next door. It appeared to the Street brothers that the Shell workers had taken the radioactive material and frantically dumped it next door in the neighboring farmer's watermelon patch in the hope of fooling the brothers-turned-environmental-sleuths. Despite the fact that the material was known to be soluble and able to enter the food chain, the Shell workers decided the best place to dump this material was in a farmer's field.

Let the games begin!

In their excitement as they reported the find that night, I realized that the amateurs, in their zeal, had very likely sunk Shell's battleship. If the Street brothers could show a jury that Shell had attempted a cover-up, the jury would see right through Shell. It seemed to Ron and me as we marveled at the Streets' gumption that the incident at Tallahala Creek did speak to something significant. At this point in 1989, it was no longer breaking news that the oil-drilling pipe was highly radioactive. Yet Shell and the other oil giants were clearly still acting as if they had something to hide.

Why? For the Streets and their employees to win a large judgment in this negligence lawsuit against their customers, they would have to prove two things: 1) that exposure to the radiation had not only forced the Street facility out of business but that radiation illness had also made workers sick, and 2) that the oil companies knew ahead of time that the material they were sending to the shop was contaminated. That second piece was critical because if they could prove such wanton negligence on behalf of these mega-rich oil companies, Shell would be liable for millions of dollars in punitive damages. Remember, Winston and his workers had been drilling out the pipe for years without ever hearing there was a risk of radiation. Frankly, neither Jack nor I—lawyers who'd lived our entire lives in one of the nation's largest oil-producing states—really had much awareness before hearing of the Streets' case that oil production produced radioactive material.

Here, once again, the earthy Street brothers were a couple of chess moves ahead of everyone else. They had realized very early on that the real key to winning their case would be to document, on paper, that Big Oil had known about its radiation problem long before the middle of the 1980s. Clark, who'd worked extensively on oil rigs as a younger man, thought he had some good ideas about where to start looking. The Streets' investigation of what the oil companies knew and when they knew it would take a two-pronged approach. First, a comprehensive timeline would need to be established of what the general scientific community knew, as evidenced by the available literature. Second would be the proof—derived from the defendants' internal files—showing their specific knowledge of the problem. The first part was massively time-consuming—it required reading through a staggering number of old geology and engineering tracts in college libraries. The second part was harder—winning the right to examine the records of the energy giants in the field and at their major corporate office sites.

With time on his hands, Clark, occasionally aided by Winston, set out on a grand quest to find a smoking gun—documents about radiation, which the Streets believed existed, that would prove the existence of a cover-up by Big Oil. At first, Clark started by going through the stacks of petroleum literature at the University of Southern Mississippi, which is located in Hattiesburg, about forty-five minutes south of Laurel. For hours at a stretch, Clark sifted through dusty books, and he even got to know some of the geology professors down at USM. But some of Clark's best sources were bland, textbook-style tracts written by petroleum engineers and chemical professors in the early days of America's oil rush and in the 1940s and 1950s, when surging crude production in the Deep South fueled the nation's war effort and then the growth of suburbia. He learned that scientists had first discovered the radioactive gas radon in 1900, in a flurry of excitement over Marie Curie's discovery of radium, a new element. By 1904 radon was detected in natural gas. Since radon was known to be produced by decay of radium, the implication was that radium could be found in rock formations containing oil and gas.

What Clark had learned from these forgotten geology and earth-science tomes was that the issue of radioactivity and oil production was well-known for decades within the ivory towers of academia—but that knowledge never trickled down to the blue-collar guys who got their hands dirty, who came home with silty radium-226 clinging to their overalls. He even found a paper at Southern Miss suggesting that one of Exxon's predecessor companies knew about radiation problems back in the 1920s. In 1954, a major geological study found large amounts of radium in the soil in Kansas oil fields, confirming reports of radioactive scale in the region.

Gradually, Clark widened his search to places like Houston, where most of the major American oil companies had headquarters—and where he hoped to prove that corporate executives were just as familiar with the latest discoveries in radiation science, yet weren't sharing that information with their contractors. That was the evidence that could convince a jury to punish Big Oil, to award millions of dollars in damages to the Streets and to their former employees.

Today, Clark looks back on those years as a remarkable time in his life. He recalls how he started doing his research when Stanford Young was still the lead attorney on the case. "I took his black

Cadillac Fleetwood and went to Houston," he said. "Then I took it to Chicago, and drove so fast that I knocked the 'd' off—so after that we called it the Fleetwoo!"

It was in Houston—where Chevron had its key regional office for the South—that Clark was really starting to hit pay dirt. "I got a lot of documents from Chevron," he said. "That was where I got this one document that they had tried to hide . . . so I 'confiscated' it."

The whole thing sounded a bit crazy back when I first heard what they were doing. For one thing, while Clark and Winston were remarkable technicians, they didn't have advanced training in engineering or the science of petro-physics. Heck, they didn't even have college degrees. In fact, I'd never heard of the actual plaintiffs in a lawsuit doing this kind of sophisticated discovery; typically that would be the work of an attorney or a paralegal or—in a complicated case like this—a consultant with highly specialized knowledge.

Of course, I already knew that the Streets had no patience for attorneys, especially the ones who seemed ready and eager to settle for a quick buck or two. But the real problem was that it sounded like they were looking for the proverbial needle in a haystack—proof of a sophisticated cover-up buried deeply amid stacks of mind-numbingly dull paperwork in dingy college libraries and fancy corporate high-rises.

ON THE GAMMA-RAY TRAIL

The pace of the informal investigation quickened once the Street brothers gained more access to at least some of Chevron's corporate files in Houston. There was something of a "Eureka!" moment when Clark located the first of many of what I would call "smoking-gun memos" buried in those files from November 29, 1982, written by one L. Max Scott, who was a radiation health expert for Gulf Oil, which was merged into Chevron two years later.

Scott reported that there had been some unusually high radiation readings posted in the company's wells near Bolton, Mississippi—in the area where pipe was shipped to the Streets for cleaning. In the memo, Scott claimed that the radiation emanating from the wellhead itself probably didn't pose a health hazard to workers—but at the same time he said the readings were troubling enough that they should be reported to Mississippi state health officials, and care should be taken when opening the pipes.

Scott wrote, "I recommend that the Mississippi State Board of Health be informed that radiation levels significantly above normal background have been observed. If you desire, I can draft a letter of notification or contact them personally."

The state's board of health was Eddie Fuente's beat; that was the outfit that would eventually show up at the Streets' yard four years later, when the radiation reports started getting too hot (pun intended) for even the oil industry to ignore. But clearly nothing ever came of Scott's recommendation. When we asked Fuente about the memo, he expressed genuine surprise, saying that he had never heard of Max Scott and that certainly he would have investigated sooner if the problem had been reported to him in 1982.

Eventually, a *New York Times* reporter tracked down Scott—by the end of the 1980s he was the radiation safety officer at my alma mater, Louisiana State University, and working for the oil companies as a TERM (technological-enhanced radioactive material) litigation consultant—and Scott insisted that he had, in fact, called Fuente's department, but he couldn't recall who he had spoken to. It seemed like Scott's intent had been sincere, but his report had likely been buried by higher-ups who didn't want his research to become public knowledge.

It's easy to see why Big Oil would want to cover up the health impacts of radium-226, one of the most dangerous and persistent forms of radiation around. To begin with, it has a half-life of more than 1,600 years. It emits both alpha and gamma radiation. Because it behaves very much like calcium, it is easily absorbed by human bone, often to a debilitating effect. Furthermore, during the process of radio-active decay, it produces the dense gas called radon, another danger-ous substance. On land or in the sea, radium-226 can very easily enter the food chain, providing yet another path to human illness.

The deeper that Clark got into his research, the more he learned that all kinds of alarm bells about radium-226 were starting to go off at Chevron—and presumably its rivals in the oil patch—in the early 1980s, around the time of the Max Scott memos and the detailed reports of radiation from the North Sea. And one name popped up again and again.

The man's name was Steve Ellington. This Chevron engineer's name had turned up in many key reports from the North Sea at the start of the 1980s. It was there, we had learned, that the big oil com-panies first began to grasp that they had a serious problem with radi-ation. Their devices that used radiation to locate oil deposits under the sea floor were acting haywire...because so much radioactive scale had already been brought back to the surface. Ellington was one of the main engineers tasked with addressing this problem.

Later Chevron decided to bring him home to the United States, re-assigning him to the Mississippi region. Then, something strange happened in the paper trail. As the Streets looked through the com-pany's local files, here was Steve Ellington again, this time filing a flurry of reports about radiation in the months before the mysterious 1986 visit from Chevron staffers out to the brothers' yard in Laurel. His name appeared on so many pieces of key paperwork that—even though they'd never met him—the Street brothers told us the engi-neer was now a running joke between the two.

We laughed around the kitchen table about the conversations that had to be taking place among his higher-ups at corporate headquar-ters: "This guy Ellington...what a pain in the ass!" We wondered if

Ellington began to feel paranoid, like maybe his bosses would probably rather kill the messenger than deal with his message of radioactivity problems.

What the Streets had figured out by following the paper trail is that when Ellington got assigned to a location called the Central Oil well site 5-6 in the Raleigh oil field in rural Mississippi, he started going through the files and noticed the exact same gamma log problem that he'd seen in the North Sea. As the brothers sifted through the Chevron papers in Houston, they located memos from Ellington to his superiors back at corporate headquarters in San Francisco, informing them that he'd be damned if he wasn't seeing the exact same radiation problems as in Europe, the ones that had cost the company so much money to remediate overseas. We had substantial evidence to believe that some older hands at Chevron knew what Ellington did not—that these high gamma readings had been occurring in Mississippi for decades.

PLEDGING THE NUCLEAR FRATERNITY

The complex discovery in the Street case was certainly an important lesson for me. That lesson, quite simply, is that knowledge is power. If I was going to face Chevron, its skilled lawyers, and their world-class consultants in a courtroom, we would need to get the right information during the discovery process and then cut through their obfuscation in front of the judge and jury. To do that, I would have to think as much like a nuclear physicist as an attorney. Fortunately, I was a young lawyer, still not that far removed from law school, and I was eager to learn.

I was barely twenty-eight when I tackled the Street case, and like any twentysomething I was eager to balance my suddenly more interesting career with the art of having a good time. For one thing,

I was in love. I had met Barry J. Cooper Jr. while we were living in the same luxury apartment building on St. Charles Avenue in New Orleans. St. Charles is the most famous street outside the French Quarter in New Orleans—oak-lined, picturesque, with the streetcar as an ever-present attraction. During Mardi Gras it's the epicenter of the parades that roll down the street day and night; my apartment was Party Central. I lived in the penthouse, having moved there after settling a big auto accident case two years before. Barry lived on the floor below. We met waiting for the elevator and it was love at first sight. After a year or so living the high life together, we decided to settle down, and have been together ever since. When I began to work on the Street case, Barry and I lived in an apartment on Lake Avenue in Metairie, the suburb just to the west of New Orleans. I wasn't rich, but I was starting to make a decent living as a young attorney, decent enough that I was looking for ways to show off my big ambitions for the future.

One day, Jack Harang—who was doing very, very well in those years—mentioned he was looking to sell his Porsche 928, and I took it off his hands for a bargain basement price. It was a burgundy two-seater with a sunroof. That Porsche turned my flat, boring, swampy drive up to Laurel into a blissful odyssey. The freedom of the open road on I-59 was an escape from some of the everyday drudgery. With the sunroof open on warm spring mornings, I searched for New Wave tunes on the radio and thought about the Street case and all its possibilities—not only to win justice but also to make my name as an attorney, opening up a brand-new field of environmental case law.

The novelty of the Street case didn't free me completely from the legal busywork that pays the bills from month to month—the personal injury and maritime law cases that were the bread and butter of Jack's practice. What's more, I knew that I'd be taking a huge risk if and when the Street case came to trial, that when I stopped working on other cases there'd be no money coming in the front door, possibly for many months. Whenever I had a spare moment, I read up on radiological health or consulted with experts who would be helpful to our case up in Laurel.

The turning point, for me, was traveling to Atlanta to defend the deposition of the Streets' radiation expert, the legendary physicist Karl Morgan. He had been a pioneer of the Atomic Age in World War II's Manhattan Project and at the storied nuclear laboratories at Oak Ridge, Tennessee, but later became a leading critic of nuclear power and its effect on human health. Although he was known as the father of health physics, I came to find out that he, like many others after him, was ostracized by the radiation community because he refused to toe the government and industry line that there were safe levels of radiation below which there would be no health effect. This mantra has now been completely discredited, and it is now recognized that any radiation exposure carries a risk. Morgan was the first radiation whistleblower, coming decades before Karen Silkwood. He paid a very high price for his integrity. After retirement he began working as an expert for injured radiation victims. He was the first but not the last real life hero I met in the radiation wars between those who believed in protecting the public and those who worked for the government-industrial complex.

When I got to Atlanta, I saw that even when they didn't agree, these experts in radiation and the atom bomb—including the World War II–era pioneers of the Hiroshima A-bomb who were in their late seventies or maybe their eighties by then—were like some kind of elite fraternity. And I wasn't a member...not yet, anyway. It was a brutal deposition. Morgan had testified in a number of radiation lawsuits and Chevron by now had realized the importance of the case and brought in Ralph Johnson, the pro-government, pro-industry dean of radiation law. He beat up on Morgan for three days, and I realized that I was in deep. I was going to have to learn even more of the science of health physics to catch up—and I was going to have to do it in a hurry.

I had not studied much hard science in college at LSU, but my major interest was philosophy, from which all sciences derive. I had taken some physics to give me a basic foundation on which to build—and my passion for mastering the details of the Street case and the intricacies of oil-patch radiation carried me the rest of the way. What's more, I knew that Jack would never do the homework that would be needed to grill nuclear experts on the witness stand. That was all on me, but it was a challenge I gladly accepted. A part of me understood that this could be the niche I was looking for: a trial lawyer for poisoned workers and dumped-on property owners who actually understood radiation science.

It was a lot harder to get up to speed back then—remember, there was no Internet yet, at least not for the masses. The most high-tech device that we used in preparing the case was a scanner. Meanwhile, my efforts to learn all the relevant literature was helped by my near-photographic memory, but almost ruined by what charitably might be called my lack of organizational skills. Recalls Clark Street: "Back then, you could hand Stuart a document and say, 'Look at this—this is what it says.' He'd say, 'Uh-huh.' Look at it, then throw it behind him, throw it behind his chair. Three weeks later, it was guaranteed that I'd be back behind the chair, looking through the pile for that damn paper."

CONSPIRACY OF SILENCE

In the months after our fateful first meeting with the Street brothers, the other cases I was working on for Jack began to fade to the back of my mind. My underdog fighting spirit had kicked in. As I sat in our small downtown New Orleans office, building the case against

Chevron and Shell, two of the world's most powerful corporations, became a nonstop obsession. I spoke with Winston or Clark, or both, on the telephone almost every day. It was an attorney-client relationship unlike anything I had ever learned about in law school—and not like anything I've seen in all of the years since then. Winston and Clark were the army of skilled investigators that we couldn't afford to hire. Ron Hirsch continued to work on the basics, such as tracking down potential witnesses.

But the Street brothers became our secret weapon, our backwoods, street-smart (again, pun intended) private eyes—even as the defendants like Chevron had the financial wherewithal and the connections to call on some of the world's top authorities on radiation, some going back to the pioneering World War II–era of atomic research at Los Alamos and elsewhere. Indeed, the more that the Streets and I advanced past our entry-level training in radiation, the more we learned about the key players in the radiation field.

In addition to Steve Ellington, another name started popping up frequently in our research. This was Henry Tyrus Miller, or H.T. Miller, and we came to learn that Miller was not just a company adviser to Chevron and other Big Oil companies on the reports of radioactive oil waste that emerged in Mississippi in the mid-1980s. It turned out that Miller had been a key player in developing the worldwide oil industry's strategy in fighting back—and preserving profits—as the extent of the radioactivity problem started to leach out into the public's consciousness at the start of the decade. Miller had a whole secret history, the complete details of which were still unknown to us in 1989, but which would in time prove critical to us in building our broader indictment of the oil industry and exactly what and when Big Oil knew about radioactivity.

Once it became clear that Miller was the expert who Chevron seemed to dispatch to put out its radium fires, we pressed Chevron and obtained court orders requiring it to hand over any and all documents that Miller had produced. We were hoping that his files could prove that Chevron had been aware of high levels of radiation and had sought to dispose of the problem long before the Street pipe yard was closed down in 1986. But the initial batch of papers that were turned over to us contained little information of any consequence.

This was the state of the case in 1989, after three years and a trail of fired lawyers: tantalizing, but not much more, not yet. We had theories; we just needed the evidence to prove them. To ask a jury for punitive damages it was critical that we showed wanton negligence by the oil companies. That's where the real dollars come into play.

Our major theory of the case was that at some point—at least in the early-to-mid-1980s but probably before that—the real dangers of radium-226 pollution suddenly became clear to Big Oil. And paying the real cost of cleaning up its radioactive waste, to the tune of billions of dollars, was not their preferred option. The biggest problem was pipe-cleaning yards like the Streets' in Laurel and dozens of others much like it, because the highly concentrated scale was where the highest radioactivity readings were recorded.

Part of our theory of the case was that the oil industry was running what amounted to a conspiracy of silence about what its radiation experts like H.T. Miller knew, and that it wanted its true awareness of its radium-226 problem to remain a secret. It was becoming clear why Shell and Chevron had offered the Streets and their original low-energy attorneys a quick down-and-dirty settlement to make the case go away: They had desperately wanted to avoid this in-depth discovery process we were now engaged in. Teamed up with me and Ron Hirsch and Jack Harang, Winston and Clark Street were rapidly becoming Big Oil's worst nightmare. But we were still nowhere near finding all the smoking guns we needed. This is where Big Oil was hoping to wear us down. To finish the job that Winston and Clark had started was going to require

Ron Hirsch (sitting) and Jack Harang hard at work.

a massive investment of time and money. Even as we continued to press, they were hoping we'd settle.

The radioactive contamination of the Streets' yard was not an isolated mistake or a random act of negligence. The callous handling of the scale-lined pipe—not to mention the massive quantities of radium-laced produced water—and the failure to properly protect workers or warn them of the health risks was instead a standard industry practice, carried out across the United States and all around the globe. A jury verdict against Big Oil and the public testimony from experts about the radioactive risks of oil production would be big news, creating a massive industry-wide liability problem as well as costly disposal techniques going forward, that could run into the billions of dollars. A settlement, even a generous one, could help the oil giants achieve their current strategy of preventing the burgeoning radioactivity issue from becoming a costly, full-blown crisis and a PR nightmare that would cut into their massive profits.

There were times when the pressure of the case got to be too much. In a recent reunion with Winston and Clark, they reminded me of one of those times, in October 1989, during the week that a California earthquake rattled the World Series. Jack and I were working on another case together up in Jackson, Mississippi, and I had summoned the Streets to visit us for a meeting. When they got there, something—I can't really recall the exact details—really set me off.

"I'm tired of this shit," Winston recalls me saying, getting more agitated. "I want to settle this damn thing and get out of it—I wanna get out of it!"

Winston also recalls shouting back, "I'll shoot yo' ass if you try."

It's always good to have the confidence of your clients.

A significant form of relief did come not too long after that. One of the two defendants, Shell, came to us seeking a settlement; this time, we advised the Streets to accept the deal, and they OK'd it. It was a smart move for all. There's an old maxim that the first guys to settle get out cheaper, and for Shell the undisclosed deal was certainly smarter economics than the expense of preparing for what was shaping up as a lengthy legal ordeal. Shell's counsel—Ed Pickle, a/k/a "Picklepatch"—wanted nothing to do with a protracted trial in Hattiesburg, Mississippi.

For us, it was a savvy monetary move: cutting a deal with Shell would ensure we had enough money to build a more solid case against Chevron, that we could finance the pre-trial discovery work without going tens of thousands of dollars into the hole.

But if the Shell settlement made sense, then why did we not reach a similar deal with Chevron? There were a couple of factors that caused this icon of Big Oil to see things differently. Chevron's top executives decided that they could break us financially (and maybe even spiritually) by dragging us into a protracted pre-trial spending war. We called it their "scorched earth policy." It was a risky strategy on their part, but if it worked, the oil giant would have squelched similar lawsuits from the other pipe-cleaning yards that it did business with. They may have felt that anything short of a decisive win in the courtroom would have opened the legal floodgates.

From our perspective, it made sense—up to a point, anyway—to go after Chevron because they had been the Streets' number-one customer. That meant the potential damages were greater, but the cost of going to trial was roughly the same as with Shell.

For me, there was little doubt about pushing the case toward trial. My father had been gone for several years now, but the gambler's genes that he had passed on to me were never very far from the surface. Maybe it was because I was young and a little foolish, or at least I didn't know how hard the oil companies could push back. Luckily I had found a kindred spirit in Jack, who was wise enough to see the potential along with the risk. And Winston and Clark were more than game—after getting knocked out of business they were spoiling for a fight.

The only problem was...so was Chevron.

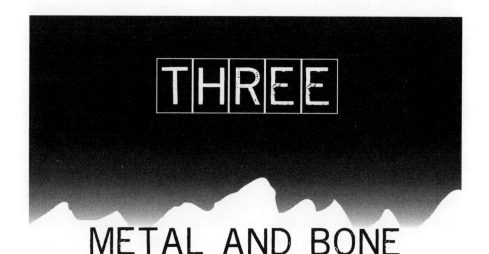

THREE

METAL AND BONE

I T WAS THE SUDDEN SNAP of bone, in a young pregnant woman, that reminded us all what was at stake in Laurel.

For roughly a decade, Winston Street's extended family—his brother, his wife and kids, nieces and nephews, plus the several dozen people who'd worked for him at Street, Inc.—hadn't just worked amid radioactive scale, the harmless-looking white dust that they'd rattled out of so many miles of oil pipe. They came home caked in the stuff, on their clothes and in their hair. The traces were everywhere—even on their living room floor. But nobody thought a thing about it until a day in October 1986 changed everything.

Karen Street was Winston's daughter-in-law—she was just twenty-six years old at the time, married to his son Michael, and six months pregnant with their first child. On this day, she sat on the edge of the bathtub in her home in Laurel, and her hip split in two.

"It was the damnedest thing," Winston told me after it happened. Karen hadn't even worked at the pipe-rattling yard. The young couple had been living on a separate eight-acre property up the road from the main shop, but there had been a time during the oil boom of the early 1980s when Winston had so much business that he performed two or three large jobs on the remote site, because he needed the extra real estate. This, of course, was during the years when the Streets were blissfully unaware of the dangers of radioactive scale.

Indeed, during the two-and-a-half years that Karen had lived on the family parcel, they raised vegetables in the backyard, normally a mark of healthy Southern eating, but not in this case. At some point after the Streets learned of the radioactive contamination of the main yard, they eventually tested the other eight-acre property up the road and learned that the soil where the vegetables had grown had been severely tainted with radiation. Indeed, they measured with a Geiger counter and got back a reading of 3,100 microrems per hour, or 310 times above background radiation levels. By way of comparison, the International Commission on Radiological Protection recommends limiting artificial irradiation of the public to an average of 100 millirems of effective dose...per year from all sources. Exposure to that level for thirty hours would exceed the recommended limit.

But at the time, Karen's bone fracture was such a bizarre accident for a young mother-to-be that her family didn't even realize at first that it was due to the radiation poisoning. It was only after I came onto the lawsuit that we hired a radiation expert and medical doctor to examine the Streets and the workers at the pipe yard. Dr. Thomas Callender confirmed that Karen was suffering from severe radium-induced bone necrosis, undoubtedly linked to her exposure to the radioactive gunk that had traveled all the way from the oil patch to her backyard. Ultimately, doctors had to put three pins in her hip to hold it together. The good news for Karen was that it was not an immediate life-threatening illness. The bad news was that the

shocking incident only served to amplify the very real, and ongoing, health worries for the workers from the Street facility and their
families.

A couple of years later, as we were taking the case against Chevron
to trial, Karen went on national PBS's *MacNeil-Lehrer Report* to talk
about her ordeal. She told the interviewer that she was frightened for
her husband, Michael Street, who had received much greater exposure to the radioactive scale while working at the machine shop—
not to mention her children, who had played in their yard. "I want
to see 'em grow up, you know," she said in the interview. "I'm trying
to raise 'em to be decent human beings and I want to see the result
of that. I have doubts that I may not see 'em grow up or Michael may
not see 'em grow up."

She wasn't the only one who was spooked by nagging ailments
that might have proved more perplexing before the radium-226 discovery. In preparing the case for trial, I met plaintiff Dusty Todd, a
thirty-year-old machinist who worked for eight years at Street, Inc.
Dusty has been incapacitated for years by severe pain in the bones in
his hips and hands. Doctors confirmed that his condition was caused
by exposure to radiation from handling radioactive pipe.

Clifton Walker, a thirty-one-year-old machinist who worked at
the Street yard for six years, has a similar debilitating condition. "I
feel like I'm sixty," he said. "I can hardly move when I get up in the
morning."

These conditions were disturbing but not surprising. Our testing
of the Street facility suggested that the workers there were exposed
to doses of radiation that were far greater than those for workers at
the Grand Gulf Nuclear Power Plant, not far away in Port Gibson,
Mississippi. The difference, of course, was that work at the nuclear
plant was heavily regulated by the federal government, so that the
employees there had to wear protective gear and were closely moni-
tored for any instances of overexposure to radiation. Conversely, the

Street employees had no idea what they were dealing with. Heck, their idea of "protective gear" probably amounted to wearing an Ole Miss baseball cap.

And so while breathing that chalky air, these men were exposing themselves daily to a radioactive payload; they dumped the deadly debris on open, unlined pits or sometimes it was even used to crudely pave back roads along with a mix of gravel or crushed shells. By then, the world was more than four decades into an Atomic Age, and society had collected a lot of information about the illnesses that had plagued workers at uranium mines, in addition to the information gleaned by what had happened to the hundreds of thousands of residents of Hiroshima and Nagasaki ravaged by the atomic blasts that ended World War II. Yet none of the volumes of accumulated knowledge about exposure to radioactivity was passed on to these blue-collar workers simply trying to earn a dollar and support their families in the American heartland.

Now, after a decade of exposure, these Mississippians faced a new psychological terror: their newfound knowledge of the potential health risks. To those who know the grim history of radioactivity in America, it felt like history was repeating itself.

ECHOES OF THE "RADIUM GIRLS"

In the years immediately after World War I, an Illinois-based firm called U.S. Radium grew as a supplier of glow-in-the-dark luminous paints mixed with the radioactive substance, accumulating lucrative contracts as a supplier of radio-luminescent watches to the U.S. military. To paint the faces of these watches, the company hired women who eventually became famous as the "Radium Girls." They handled the job with no warning of the potential health risks (which were known, of course, to U.S. Radium's scientists and supervisors, even back then). And so, remarkably, they often twisted their toxic paint-brushes with their lips to keep a fine point on the bristles, or painted their nails or even their teeth with the glowing radium to make a fashion statement.

It was not long before the Radium Girls developed an array of debilitating illnesses. One of the worst was called "radium jaw," the slow destruction of the upper and lower jaws that began with bleeding gums and usually resulted in tumors, bone decay, and severe deformity. Other illnesses linked to radium exposure include weakening and decay of the bones as well as anemia, fractured teeth, and elevated rates of cancer. In the case of U.S. Radium, company officials worked overtime to cover up cases of sickness and death or to blame other factors (including, in a cruel, crude, and proto-sexist assault on the young female workers, syphilis). But over time, their case established new standards for workplace safety.

I couldn't help but wonder if the pipe-rattlers of Laurel, Mississippi, were the "Radium Boys" of the latter twentieth century. In the time since the gates had been padlocked at Street, Inc., we'd started seeing exactly the kind of early medical reports that we'd feared: necrosis and other bone illnesses, anemia and fatigue, and premature aging. The worry was growing and it was taking quite a psychological toll on the former Street employees and their families. It seemed like the big oil companies had behaved somewhat like U.S. Radium had done a half-century earlier—shielding workers from knowledge about the dangers they faced, and then denying any connection once people started getting sick.

But there was another, even crueler part of the story that started to emerge, and once again it was the crafty Street brothers who played the lead in exposing the connection. Pipe-cleaning yards had emerged in the late 1980s as the ground zero of the oil industry's radiation crisis, for obvious reasons. By rattling the pipe and loosening up the radioactive scale inside, the dust and chalky gunk they broke free was the material that threatened the workers' health—but when they were done the pipes were clean as a whistle inside. The production pipes that they cleaned were returned to the oil patch, where the cycle of energy production (and radium pollution) took place all over again. But eventually, miles and miles of worn-out and aging pipe, hot from residual radioactive scale, had to be retired and replaced.

Where did all this old pipe go?

From their years working in the Mississippi oil patch, Winston and Clark had a rough idea of the answer. They believed they had found supporting evidence that much of the spent, radioactive pipe—material that typically emitted levels of radiation that should have triggered careful monitoring by the federal Nuclear Regulatory Commission and that should have been disposed in a licensed landfill for radioactive waste—was simply dumped out in open fields across the Southern woods, piled high in large stacks that concentrated the dangerous gamma radiation.

But even unregulated and hazardous dumping sometimes proved too great a chore for the cost-cutting, time-saving field generals of Big Oil. Their preferred method of dealing with these hot pipes was quite simply to give them away. The long metal tubes were, unfortunately, well-suited to be recycled and repurposed on land, often as part of metal fencing or barriers.

Even before Jack and I came onto the case, the Street brothers had developed an obsession with tracing the whereabouts of the pipe that the oil companies had given away. In one sense, it was more proof of their remarkable, God-given ability as environmental private eyes. After all, even though it had nothing directly to do with the radioactive contamination of the Streets' property, if they could prove that the energy firms like Chevron knew all about the health hazards contained inside of their pipe and yet continued to distribute it into the community by poisoning the places where their workers and their customers strolled or played ball, it would help their case in court. It would show not just carelessness but gross negligence by Big Oil, well beyond the pollution that occurred at the machine shop. More importantly, Winston and Clark were acting in good faith, as solid citizens of Mississippi. If there was radioactive material in the local parks or schoolyards, they wanted to see it removed so that no one else would get sick or have to worry, like Winston's daughter-in-law had.

Clark didn't have to look very hard to uncover his first major case of contamination. The Beat Four Elementary School was off U.S. 84 in Waynesboro, Mississippi, just a couple of miles east of Laurel. It was where Clark had learned his ABCs as a small child back in the 1950s, and he still traveled by his old school frequently. So when they'd built a gleaming new fenced-in ball field at the Beat Four school, he was already well aware that the field had been enclosed with discarded pipe from the oil patch.

In 1986, fuming over the shutdown of the pipe-rattling yard, Clark decided he was going to check out the metal fence at the Beat Four field where dozens of kids played ball every day. One afternoon he drove out there with his new toy, the Geiger counter that he'd also used to find the pipe he believed that Shell had dumped in the watermelon patch. Sure enough, the needle started spinning as he came up a walkway that was lined with the recycled pipe for railings and support. He immediately contacted Eddie Fuente at the state health department. Mississippi had a big problem.

Unsurprisingly, all hell broke loose. Radioactive oil pipes found in schools made front-page headlines all across Mississippi. State officials ordered every single school in the Magnolia State to conduct a thorough investigation into whether radioactive spent pipe from the oil patch had been donated and put to use anywhere on school grounds. Remarkably, some twenty-two schools across the oil patch discovered places where the hot pipe was in use; it was found on the playgrounds where kids spent their recess, on the ball fields where they practiced after school, and lining the paths where they walked toward the schoolhouse door. Some of the old pipes and equipment that were recycled in schools or other public buildings were found to emit radiation levels 800 times above background levels. As one newspaper report noted, "If someone stood close to these pipes for four hours, they would receive as much radiation as one bone X-ray." In another instance, it was discovered that these old radioactive pipes were being used to train new welders who were cutting them up in their classrooms at Mississippi's vocational schools, which exposed their lungs to the radioactive dust in the process.

The school officials were ordered to immediately spray paint any metal that tested positive for radiation a bright orange, and to rip it out and haul it away as soon as possible. But in a foreshadowing of the battles ahead, Mississippi could not even get that simple task right.

When Clark returned to the affected schools, he saw that the orange-painted pipe had indeed been removed, but the other tubing that had been donated by the oil companies was still standing. Did the officials not realize that all of the used pipes were lined with scale contaminated with radium-226, and thus a potential risk?

When Clark and the reporter from PBS walked up to the Beat Four school, they saw kids picking and eating the wild blackberries that were growing under the fence right where it had just been cut open; he was furious because, he explained, it was his third visit to the school and the pipe was still there. "And I mean it's the kind of things that they tell you we've taken care of this mess, you can rest assured your children are safe," Clark told the national television audience.

Fuente was irate over the botched work as well. "If it's open-ended and where they removed certain, just a part, part of a section of pipe—it's open-ended, and the scale is falling to the ground, well, it just makes the problem much larger," he said. Years later,

Clark would tell me that a lot of that hot pipe is still standing at the Beat Four Elementary School today, painted orange in some spaces but still not removed. It's been a similar story at a number of other Mississippi sites that were uncovered either by Clark's initial digging or the subsequent state investigation led by Fuente.

What the Street case had done was open up a spider's web of trouble across the South. State officials across the oil-producing states of the Gulf Coast read the news accounts out of Mississippi and stepped up their own investigations of the TERM problem, starting at pipe yards like the Streets' but expanding to look at the same problem of radioactive pipe where little children played. Just over the border in Louisiana, where oil production had skyrocketed in the late 1970s and early 1980s, the director of the state Department of Environmental Quality (DEQ), Dr. Paul Templet, was dealing with significant radiation problems.

"We also did some testing, and some of our people went out and measured radiation from pipes that had been donated to playgrounds in schools, and things like that," Templet explained in a recent interview. "So when this pipe was not usable anymore, they would just give it away. And one of my guys told me that if you sat on one of these pipes for about an hour, you could get your yearly dose of radiation. We had to stop the movement." For a brief, shining moment, the normally conservative, pro-business state of Louisiana was leading the nation in environmental protection for TERM, in these years where Big Oil was briefly caught flat-footed.

A TOXIC MORNING IN REAGAN'S AMERICA

Indeed, the role of a handful of aggressive state regulators in states such as Mississippi and Louisiana—not exactly famous as bastions of green, granola-crunchy environmentalism—was critical in the mid-to-late 1980s. That's because Washington, D.C. had all but completely abrogated its responsibility to protect its citizens from industrial abuses during the presidency of Ronald Reagan, who had a not-so-secret agenda to roll back the environmental gains of the 1970s. Throughout the decade, Reagan's EPA and its eventually disgraced leader Anne Gorsuch Burford made headlines by reducing the number of agents and taking brazen steps to protect toxic polluters. By 1986, Gorsuch Burford was gone but the EPA's innate hostility to its supposed mission of environmental protection was still there.

This was a source of tremendous frustration to dedicated regulators such as Mississippi's Fuente, who had quickly reached the conclusion that the problem of cleaning up TERM-contaminated sites in his state was clearly something that surpassed the capacity of his small and overworked department. To the state's top radiation regulator, the only viable solution was to ask the EPA to get involved and to declare properties like the Street pipe-rattling yard as a Superfund site and force the oil companies not only to restore them to their original condition but to transport the tainted soil to a hazardous-waste facility. Fuente wrote the following to federal regulators at the tail end of the 1980s:

"The oil and gas production states sharing this potential problem need assistance from the U.S. Environmental Protection Agency (EPA) in the establishment of radiation protection standards. The control and disposal of radioactive contaminated oil and gas production tubing and the associated deposition of naturally occurring radioactive materials [NORM] in the form of scale must be regulated."

Fuente noted that he had contacted the EPA before, to no avail:

"In May and August, 1986, EPA's assistance was requested through Messrs. Sheldon Meyers and Jack Evans, respectively, but to date, EPA has not given the proper attention to this developing public health issue. By no means is this radioactive contamination problem unique to Mississippi, but one which is common with any oil and gas production state."

The EPA had a blind spot, and you didn't need a Ph.D. in political science to understand what it was. During the 1980s, the federal government spent tens of millions of dollars warning the public about radon contamination in homes, but not a red cent on educating people about the dangers of TERM. That's because the radon that plagued homeowners in the Northeastern United States truly was naturally occurring, and raising public awareness didn't harm any businesses, while aggressively attacking radioactivity in the oil patch would have lopped hundreds of millions of dollars off of the oil company profits. And Big Oil had heavily funded the successful presidential campaigns of Ronald Reagan, while the next occupant of the Oval Office, George H.W. Bush, was a former Texas oilman.

But the publicity about radioactivity in and around schools, all the result of Clark and Winston's detective work, was priceless, because it was accomplishing the thing that Big Oil truly feared the most: It was making the industry's radium-226 issue into a national story. The biggest public relations nightmare would be an article in the *New York Times*, the one newspaper that was read religiously by congressmen and senators in Washington, by the regulators in the top-floor offices of the EPA, by environmental journalists and activists around the nation, and of course, by the board members and the top executives of the oil companies like Chevron. On December 3, 1990, the story they feared was splayed across the *Times* front page: "Radiation Danger Found in Oilfields Across the Nation."

For me, the story—which began by stating, "Radium from the earth's crust has been brought to the surface in decades of oil drilling, causing widespread radioactive contamination of the nation's oilfields"—was not exactly breaking news. I'd been living the story for more than a year, since the Streets had asked Jack and me to take on their case. The information it conveyed must have been a real eye-opener to many other people.

The article by the *Times*' Keith Schneider noted the complete lack of federal and state regulations to deal with the problem, which seemed to be worse along the Gulf Coast than elsewhere. It also chronicled, with some alarm, how wastewater with levels of radioactivity that would trigger all sorts of protective measures at a federally regulated nuclear power plant had routinely been dumped into unlined pits in the oil fields.

The explosive *Times* article quoted Louisiana's Dr. Paul Templet: "When I got here in 1988, this radium contamination in the oil fields was the only environmental problem that I had never heard about. At first I didn't believe it. But we investigated it, found out it was true and now it's our newest environmental problem." Louisiana's top regulator added a warning to Big Oil, that they "can no longer use the environment as a free disposal system."

After I'd scrambled to find a copy of that morning's *Times* on the streets of New Orleans, I felt a rush of excitement, but also a lump of anxiety. The article not only mentioned the Street brothers' case but also noted that our lawsuit was scheduled to come to trial in March 1991—little more than three months away—at the federal courthouse in Hattiesburg in the heart of southern Mississippi.

It crossed my mind that possibly none of this (the multistate investigations, the front-page coverage in the *New York Times*) would be happening if the Streets had taken the advice of their earlier lawyers and walked away with a quick buck. Now, I was at the epicenter of a national story. And it was going to be up to me—just thirty-one and not far removed from law school—and Jack, a skilled courtroom litigator with little patience for the complicated science of microrem exposure, with a helping hand from the Streets and a few other renegades, to try to win this complex case with the potential to shake one of America's most profitable industries to its very core.

The stakes in Laurel were laid bare in the *New York Times* article. The costs to the oil industry, if it was required to safeguard workers and dispose of wastewater under the same types of rules that govern the nuclear power industry, could run into the billions of dollars. Of course, industry officials insisted that they were going to do the right thing in the name of public safety, at least in print.

"I do not believe the oil and gas industry is going to shirk their responsibility for cleanup where it's necessary," said Buck Steingraber, a geologist for Mobil Oil who'd been put in charge of an emergency ad hoc committee by the American Petroleum Institute (API) to study the growing radiation crisis. "The question of cost is going to be determined by the standards of safety that are set by regulators." Reading between the lines, Big Oil was willing to spend millions lobbying to make sure those regulators bent in the directions of the corporations, and to knock down any worrisome legal precedents.

Sure enough, when it became clear that the case against Chevron was headed for the courtroom, the company called on the biggest gun in the field of radiation law: Ralph Johnson. Handsome and distinguished, Johnson looked like the straight-arrow corporate attorney sent down from central casting; indeed, he was, and still is, a pioneer in developing defenses—first for the federal government and later for large companies—for the heavy hitters who have stood accused of poisoning their workers in the Atomic Age. He was an expert in downplaying the risks of radiation exposure and quashing people's claims. The rumor on the street was that the federal government had a team of radiation lawyers who were trained to beat these cases at our national laboratories such as Oak Ridge National Laboratory in Oak Ridge, Tennessee. Deeply committed to his Mormon faith, Johnson was a man who not only didn't smoke or drink, but also he wouldn't touch caffeine-laced Coca-Cola when it was offered up in a deposition room.

When I think back on the times that I've crossed paths (and swords) with the imposing Johnson over the years, I think of The

Scowl. He was a humorless man who almost never smiled, but behind the grim countenance was a computer-like mind of knowledge about the invisible world of radiation.

In a strange way, Johnson inspired me to be a better lawyer. Every time we faced off across a conference table, it was clear to me how much more I would have to learn about radiation science before I caught up to him, if I ever could. It pushed me to work harder, to come home and read science books and pore through old cases while some of my young lawyer peers were out at happy hour.

Ralph Johnson was a man of the West who worked his way up through the U.S. Justice Department in Utah. A few years before the Street case, Johnson had been asked to defend the government in a high-profile lawsuit by thousands of Utah and Nevada residents who claimed they'd been poisoned by years of U.S. nuclear testing, thus establishing his *bona fides* as an expert in the field. He ultimately directed the radiation and toxic tort unit for the Justice Department. He helped to establish the framework of the courtroom defense that both government and later corporate lawyers would fall back on again and again and again.

Ultimately, we came up with a name for his legal technique: "dose dancing." To win a complicated radiation lawsuit against Chevron or any other big corporation, the conventional wisdom is that it's not enough to show that workers or community members who were exposed to radioactive material became ill, even when their ailments, like Karen Street's necrosis at such a young age, would make reasonable people surmise that there could be no other cause but radiation exposure.

What I learned in preparing for the Street case is that there is an art to being an environmental lawyer. It's a lot different from acting as your stereotypical "ambulance chaser" lawyer. For example, when you file a lawsuit in a car accident after two vehicles collide and one of the drivers breaks his neck, you don't have to spend a lot of time in court establishing the connection between the wreck and the injury. Radiation law is very different. The most serious impacts of poisoning from a substance like radium-226, such as cancer, might not show up for decades, and in the meantime, it's difficult to prove that other aches and pains are the result of exposure to radioactivity, no matter how strong the suspicion. Over time, case law established that plaintiffs had to show they were placed under "substantial risk," and that required proving there was significantly more risk of becoming ill than an average person faces. Given the high radiation readings that were recorded by Fuente and his team with the Geiger counters when they first showed up at the Street property in 1986, the average person might think that was a slam dunk.

But what lawyers like Johnson specialized in was obfuscating the issues and casting what they considered reasonable doubt, usually by unleashing a bombardment of data meant to suggest that the radiation dosage that a worker or bystander received still fell below a certain standard and was simply too low to cause an illness. This was an effective tactic because a juror could be easily confused by the conflicting numbers getting tossed about, especially when expressed in measurements like "microrems" or "picocuries," which the average person has never heard before. What's more, the scientific jargon of dose dancing had a way of blunting the raw, emotional impact of witnesses like the Street brothers, who'd lost their family business because of radium-226 contamination and were now watching former employees and family members complain of headaches, clogged sinuses, and aching bones.

As the reality of the looming trial in Hattiesburg grew closer, our team began to realize that Chevron's lawyers had the ability and the patience to use dose dancing to drag the testimony out for weeks, months, and possibly for years. This was their ace in the hole, slowing down the clock to pressure regular folks like Winston and Clark

Street to accept a settlement on Chevron's terms and to keep quiet, to continue to sweep Big Oil's problem under the rug.

Chevron had assembled its own three-pronged dream team to take on me and Jack in the courtroom. Although Johnson was clearly the superstar, the other two attorneys were key pieces in their strategy. "Mr. Inside," if you will, was the Chevron in-house lawyer working the case, David Martindale. Martindale took the case very personally, which is not uncommon among in-house trial lawyers. They are employed by the corporate defendant and as such, they usually don't have the perspective you need to objectively and dispassionately evaluate a case. Deep down, Martindale was just a nice guy who had a nasty job to do. Martindale once said about TERM victims in Brookhaven, Mississippi: "I can't believe these people are suing us. We put shoes on their feet." The air of "how dare you" permeated the defendant's side of the proceedings. "Mr. Outside" was Gene Hortman, a talented local attorney from the Streets' hometown of Laurel who knew the lay of the land in ways that Johnson and Martindale did not, and who the defense surely hoped would connect with a Mississippi jury in a way that the out-of-towners simply could not.

The judge was clearly going to be critical to the outcome. And the selection of a jurist said a lot about how the Deep South was starting to change as the 1980s, the era of Reagan and "morning in America," morphed into the 1990s. U.S. District Judge Henry T. Wingate was a true trailblazer—a native of Jackson, Mississippi, and a graduate of Yale Law School; for a time in the mid-1970s, he was the only African-American attorney in the U.S. Navy—and he had just become the first black federal district court judge in Mississippi. But Wingate was also at least nominally a Republican, having been named to the job by Reagan on the recommendation of GOP U.S. Senator Thad Cochran. Although some Republican judges show their corporate leanings on the bench, we were optimistic that Wingate would give us a fair shake.

That was crucial, because the decisions that Wingate would need to make regarding our claims about Chevron's chronic and inexcusable delay delivering documents and other evidence we believed existed would surely be as important as winning over the jury, perhaps more so. It was still our strong hunch that the papers about the effects of NORM that Clark had found in Houston and in dusty university library stacks were just the tip of the iceberg, and that Chevron and the other oil giants were likely sitting on a much larger paper trail that could establish that they knew their pipes were radioactive. The judge had ordered them to produce all such information during pre-trial discovery, and there would be hell to pay if they had not.

Two of the things we were pressing most aggressively for were the environmental test results Chevron had taken that would show the concentration of radiation in the scale clogging the pipes that were delivered to the Streets, and the "field files," which I learned initially from Clark and Winston were the detailed records that were generated by oil-field engineers at the wellhead. By now, we knew that the detailed gamma logs were what had tipped off the oil companies to the extensive radiation problem in Europe's North Sea; so why didn't similar paperwork exist for the Mississippi oil patch? It didn't add up. The only well records the oil companies allowed us to see were in the corporate headquarters in Houston.

As the trial grew closer, our frustration over the discovery process was growing palpable. Chevron had clearly taken what one might call a "minimalist" approach to the whole thing, turning over relatively paltry boxes of mostly unhelpful material. Clark and Winston were growing livid during this time. In every conversation I had with them, they insisted from their own experience working jobs in the oil patch that there should be massive cabinets full of these field files, or "field well logs."

"We kept asking for their field files, and they just kept right on denying they had them," Winston later recalled. "They would say, 'we don't have anything called field files.' And that went on for a while. We asked for them field files three and four times. The judge never pushed them too hard on it, because they denied they had them in the first place." However, the judge did order them to produce all records in their possession related to the oil fields from which tubing was extracted and cleaned by Street, Inc., and all adjacent fields.

Winston was incredulous—he swore up and down that he'd personally seen this kind of file many times. "Me and Clark went out to Soso"(a major production field in Mississippi), "and I'd worked in them files one hundred times out in that oil field because I had cleaned a lot of pipe out there," he said. "They'd call me out there to do a job and we'd look at those files from the wellhead and they'd tell you what size pipe they had out there and what the ID number was. I had to know that so I could fill the bit."

Now all those files could not be found and we weren't sure if we could win our case without them.

That wasn't the only problem that Clark Street faced. As he pushed harder for Big Oil's radioactive secrets, he felt certain he was being intimidated, maybe even threatened.

Once around midnight, after snooping around the oil patch and looking through all kinds of records for three or four years, Clark was watching late-night TV when he jerked upright to a loud screech outside, and the sound of shattering glass. About four or five shotgun rounds had been fired, including one that sailed over where his wife had been sleeping, but mostly ripping apart his car, which had been parked in the driveway at the end of his dead-end road. He was able to tell that the shots had come from a 12-gauge magnum but neither he nor the authorities ever learned who was responsible.

We have no evidence of any connection to the case, but it sure seemed like someone was trying to scare Clark.

"PARANOIA STRIKES DEEP"

The torpid pace of civil action can be a numbing thing. The world had changed significantly in the six years since the Street brothers had been shocked by the arrival of the Geiger counter brigade—by the California earthquake at home and by war in the Persian Gulf abroad, with the surge of a non-politician named Ross Perot and with a so-called "Man From Hope" named Bill Clinton looking to finally retake the White House from the Republicans. Most of the men who'd once made a decent paycheck rattling oil pipe in Laurel had long moved on; some worked as cops or in auto-body shops, some had divorced and remarried. Like a highly anticipated football game, it should have been exhilarating to finally collide, full contact, at the legal line of scrimmage with Chevron's team of lawyers and to present the case that we'd spent years documenting.

But when the Streets and I look back on that summer (it was June of 1992 when we finally went to trial), we keep coming back to the paranoia. I can't remember the exact day when we got the idea in our heads that we were being watched, that somehow, some way, Chevron's legal team had a way of finding out our courtroom strategy practically before we did. But it was very early in the trial.

I want to be clear: What I'm about to describe here is what was going on in our own minds as the days turned into weeks in the languid, humid fog of a long hot Mississippi summer. There is absolutely no proof, then or now, that Chevron's attorneys actually did anything unethical or illegal in this regard.

But as the case of *Street v. Chevron* dragged on throughout 1992, as the long dusky nights of June slowly morphed into the nippy season when bright Christmas lights lined the ramshackle front porches near downtown Hattiesburg, the possibility that we were under some kind of surveillance ruled our conversations, dominated our every move.

It really hit home with something we called the "Coleman lantern episode."

As expected, the Chevron team led by Ralph Johnson did every-thing possible to minimize both the dosage and the significance of the radioactivity that the Streets, their relatives, and the employees had been exposed to at the pipe-cleaning yard. One of their arguments from day one was that a popular item in Mississippi, the Coleman camping lantern, was filled with a radioactive substance, thorium, for greater incandescence. Johnson made a big deal in court one day about how Coleman lantern mantles emitted radiation like the oil-field scale. That night, sitting around our rented house outside of Hattiesburg, we dispatched our investigator Ron Hirsch to run back into town and buy up a couple of Coleman lanterns so we could test them with our Geiger counter. It turned out that by 1992, because of the uproar over radioactivity, Coleman had already phased out the thorium.

The next morning, we walked into the federal courthouse with our brand-new camping lantern, ready for our small-scale "Perry Mason moment," when Johnson stood up with a well-hashed-out objection to our gambit, which was sustained by Judge Wingate. Johnson raised the objection before we even took out or mentioned the mantles. That night, we fumed. How had they known our strategy? At the time I was convinced Ron had been followed to the hardware store.

You have to understand that trial lawyers have a natural tendency to be some of the most paranoid people on Earth. When he started winning cases, often against not-the-most-reputable defendants, Jack installed a device that would be pretty common now but was quite unique at the dawn of the 1990s—a button to start his car remotely. At a safe distance, Jack would hit a button and lights would go on underneath and the engine would rev, proving that no one had snuck underneath and planted a car bomb. Jack had this installed after successfully suing a mob-connected New Jersey nursing home and then surviving an arson attack on his country home.

We had set up a base camp in southern Mississippi; to call our setup unique would truly be an understatement. We knew that our team—me, Jack, Ron, and a smart young law clerk named James Cox—would need a lot of space, not just to sleep but to hold strategy sessions or prepare key witnesses. That wouldn't be easy in Hattiesburg, where most of the accommodations are low-rent, low-rise motels that fill up a half-dozen times a year for USM football games. The judge and his staff ended up at the Holiday Inn Express and perhaps fittingly, the Chevron lawyers took over a quaint, comfortable bed-and-breakfast in town.

Like any trial lawyers worth our salt, we'd spent most everything that we'd budgeted in getting ready for the case, on trips to Houston and San Francisco to dig through records, so we needed a cheap alternative. Money was starting to become an issue; just before the trial, the telephone system in the law firm was targeted by the vendor for confiscation for delinquent account status.

At the last minute, a lawyer I knew who was married to the daughter of a former Mississippi governor mentioned an opportunity to cheaply rent some unusual digs. It was a rambling one-story cottage on a winding road way back in a park that was named for that ex-governor—Paul B. Johnson State Park—on the main highway some twenty miles south of Hattiesburg. The park was a splendid retreat in the heart of Mississippi's pine belt, shrouded thickly in flowering dogwoods and southern yellow pines. The cottage itself was large, with a massive great room with a real large fireplace and four bedrooms. It was a peaceful getaway, with its spacious patio, a gurgling fountain, and a spare servants' room out back.

We had to laugh at the irony, since the giant body of water in the center of the park had changed its name a few years back from Lake Shelby to Lake Geiger, a fitting backdrop for developing our radiation case against Chevron. What's more, the park claimed its name from—and our cottage was still technically in the hands of—one of Mississippi's most storied political families. Both Paul B. Johnson Sr., who'd been governor of the Magnolia State during World War II, and the son named for him, Mississippi's governor during the most turbulent civil-rights years of the 1960s, had been ardent segregationists. In fact, it was Paul Johnson Jr. who tried to physically block the federal marshals from enrolling James Meredith in the University of Mississippi in 1962. He then won the statehouse that fall with a stump speech that claimed the NAACP stood for "(N-word)s, alligators, apes, coons, and possums."

It may seem like a point of trivia to mention this, but our state-park hideaway was one of those reminders that are a part of daily life in the Deep South—that the struggle for civil rights runs deep in the blood-red soil. To some degree, we felt that fighting to stop working-class folks in a place like Laurel from getting dumped on by a big global corporation like Chevron was a civil-rights battle for a new generation.

Here's where the paranoia began to strike deep, as the old Buffalo Springfield tune went. Just across the winding road from the governor's cottage, down a small embankment and on the shore of the big lake was the main campground. In the first week of the trial, a large recreational vehicle pulled into the closest camping space to the cottage, just down a small hill. And this one RV stayed parked there most of the next six months, through unbearable heat waves and then into the autumn as the leaves began to fall. They must have been happy campers, because we never saw anyone emerge from the massive vehicle with the large TV dish antenna in the back.

Again—and I cannot stress this enough—the presence of this RV may have seemed as suspicious as hell but we had not one iota of proof that it had anything to do with Chevron or the trial. But what is factual, and cannot be denied, is that our increasing paranoia had a big impact on our own behavior, not to mention increasing the stress levels of the already tense situation of suing Big Oil in a federal courtroom. Every time Chevron's lawyers arrived at court seemingly aware of and overprepared for our next move, which happened on more than one occasion, our paranoia increased. Did they have inside information or were they just really smart?

Was it possible that somebody could have attached a bugging device to the big picture windows looking out on Lake Geiger, one that was powerful enough to detect our conversations in the front of the cottage? With hundreds of millions, maybe even billions, of dollars at stake in the broader TERM issue, why wouldn't Big Oil spend thousands of dollars on surveillance? So first, we started going down the road to a pay phone at the park office to make any important phone calls. Late at night, we'd take our strategy meetings out to the back of the cottage, sitting around the fountain so that the loud running water would thwart anyone trying to listen in.

Soon, Clark came down with an RV that he owned and we'd use that to prepare key witnesses, driving them to a remote corner of Paul Johnson State Park and firing our practice questions while we sat parked in the vehicle. It was our own version of *Spy vs. Spy*, conducted with dueling RVs. Like I said, maybe the cat-and-mouse stuff was all in our heads.

Maybe it was a way to add some excitement and intrigue as the actual trial in Judge Wingate's courtroom moved at a snail's pace. The spy games were just one front in a war. The main battle line of presenting testimony felt at times like the Western Front in World War I, arduous trench warfare moving inches at a time. But the real drama was the race against time taking place outside the walls of the courthouse, the race to prove, if we could, that even as the trial was underway, Chevron was still carrying out a massive cover-up.

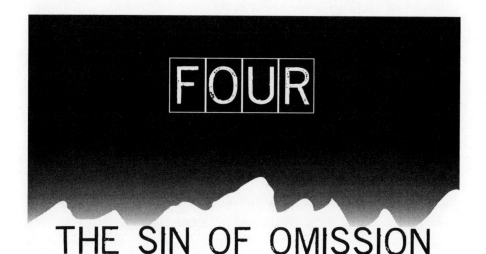

FOUR

THE SIN OF OMISSION

WHEN MOST PEOPLE THINK of a long summer trial in a place like Mississippi, *To Kill a Mockingbird* probably comes to mind, a stately white nineteenth-century palace of justice with giant ceiling fans, a packed balcony, and lawyers regally wiping the sweat off their brows.

But this was the 1990s, and so the classical old federal courthouse in downtown Hattiesburg had long ago been replaced by a modern three-story rectangular monstrosity of bone-white concrete and glass, plopped down on Main Street near the railroad tracks and the towering ivory column of the Confederate Memorial. Judge Wingate's courtroom up on the second floor was muffled by thick carpet and thick wood paneling, and by the nonstop hum of powerful central air-conditioning. It was comfortable but sometimes deathly quiet, and few spectators bothered to sit in on the long grueling cross-examinations of radiation experts. You would have never guessed the multimillion-dollar stakes for Big Oil that were playing out against the cooling drone.

As judge, Wingate played a critical role in controlling the pace of our showdown. He struck me as exceedingly fair to both sides in such a complicated matter. Maybe that reflected the tension in his own background; he grew up a black Republican, a child of civil-rights–era Jackson, Mississippi, who had found order as a military lawyer. For better or worse, an older judge with more experience might have sped the pace, as one key witness—our physician Dr. Thomas Callender, the one who diagnosed young Karen Street with radiation-induced bone necrosis—spent nearly a month on the witness stand, much of it under Johnson's grueling, nit-picking cross-examination. Watching Johnson do the "dose dance" with Dr. Callender was an amazing learning experience. He is a true artist at rhetoric and persuasion. Callender stood his own and we knew when Johnson was getting hot and irritated because his right hand would start to shake ever so slightly.

Jack had similar talents and watching them go at it was very exciting. One of the things that Jack did to drive Johnson crazy was at the beginning of trial during opening statements Jack presented a wrapped box to the jury and said that at the end of the trial he would open the box and the answers to the case would be in there. Johnson nearly went berserk wondering what was in the box.

Still, the presence of a black judge was another symbol of the hot, slow winds of change in the American South. Occasionally in Wingate's chambers, we had an opportunity to gossip about that year's presidential election; as a 1972 graduate of Yale Law School, Wingate was a classmate of both President Bill Clinton and his wife. "Bill's real smart," he confided in me once, "but Hillary's the smarter one." History has arguably proved him right.

Most of these moments of levity were off the record that summer. Our official mission was as serious as a heart attack—to move past the undeniable truth that the Streets' biggest customer, Chevron, had polluted their yard with radioactive pipe and helped drive the company out of business, to prove the much more damaging claim that a paragon of Big Oil had harmed both the physical and mental health of workers and families despite top executives' full knowledge of the harm they were creating. That last piece was critical because establishing that Chevron knew its pipes were poisonous would open the firm to millions of dollars in punitive damages for its reckless misconduct.

And so we were moving on two separate tracks. Inside the concrete fortress on Main Street in Hattiesburg, we painstakingly presented the considerable evidence we had been able to collect despite Chevron's delay tactics. Jack, with his polished yet folksy courtroom manner, had the task of examining the workers and members of the Street family who'd been exposed to the radioactive scale. With my self-taught crash course in radiation science, I was in charge of grilling the technical and medical experts. But we didn't yet have the smoking gun that would show that Chevron knew well before 1986 that it was sending hot radioactive pipe to the Streets.

When we weren't clashing over the evidence, we unfolded the testimony from our plaintiffs and some of it was heartbreaking. The stress for some of the young family members with their whole lives ahead of them and the burden of their knowledge that they'd been poisoned and were at a risk for getting sick down the road provided more powerful witness testimony than the actual ailments suffered by some of the adult workers. The jury got to see that the workers and their family members who'd had their lives turned upside down by what we claimed was wanton negligence of oil companies such as Chevron were pillars of the community, regular folks just like them.

Early in the trial, they heard from witnesses such as Douglas Knight, a then thirty-year-old police sergeant who was on the job right there in Hattiesburg. Knight had started work at the Streets' yard in Laurel when he was in high school, performing odd jobs there for about $3 an hour. Later, while still a teenager, he began working there full-time and learned to maintain the pipe-rattling equipment, ultimately spending six years there before moving on to police work when the business collapsed after the 1986 radiation discovery.

Knight told jurors that pipe rattling was "dirty, nasty" work in which he regularly breathed, ate, and even came home caked in, the chalky dust. And like most of the other former employees that we called to the stand, he was experiencing aches and pains and a lot of sinus problems, but some of the greatest trauma was inside his anguished mind.

"The thing that really scares me is I don't think anyone knows what this stuff can really do to us," Knight testified on July 28, 1992. "I'm concerned about my quality of life and how it's going to affect me in the years to come. I mean, nobody really knows if it's going to be ten, fifteen, twenty, or forty years and then suddenly show up. I'm extremely scared of cancer. I'm scared of being rendered disabled in some way. And I wonder if like—you know, I have two children, if in some ways it's going to come to affect them, in the years to come."

Indeed, looking back on the trial, it's striking what a key role was played by young people, especially the children and nieces and nephews of Winston and Clark. They offered surprising testimony to the extent that they visited their dads or other family members at the pipe yards, running around that filthy dust or even grabbing lunch there. There is no greater sin in our society than endangering a child, and the jurors learned how Chevron had done exactly that over and over again.

Some of the most moving testimony in that regard came from an employee named David Jones, who testified early in the trial, on July 20, 1992. In many ways, Jones was a typical employee of Winston's pipe-rattling yard—thirty-two years old, a son of an Air Force officer who found himself a young woman in Mississippi, got married, had three kids, got divorced, and worked long gritty hours in machine shops and auto-body shops around Laurel to support his family. He'd worked for five years as a supervisor for Street, Inc., and he said that it had been the nastiest job he'd ever worked in his life, with thick scale coating his overalls and getting in his mouth. "It has got a taste, a dirty gritty taste—it just gets in your mouth."

Jones, like everyone else who worked at the site in Laurel, testified he had no idea that the pipes that Chevron and the other oil companies trucked there were thickly lined with radium-226. But there was one occurrence that made his testimony different and quite memorable. He said that three or four days a month, he'd be so busy that his wife would drop by and bring him lunch, and she'd bring their three kids, who were toddlers at the time. He said they chased each other happily through the yard, sometimes making sand castles in the dust that no one knew was so highly radioactive. Once, he confessed to the jury, no one was keeping close enough tabs on his youngest daughter as she played.

"I had left my other two children watching her," Jones testified. "...At the time, she was two or a little bit younger than two years old. And I went to get cleaned up to get ready to go home and my wife went into the shop with me. My oldest two were supposed to be watching the little one. When we got back out there, she had stuff in her mouth and her hands just like she was eating dirt. She was sitting in a pile of it, eating it."

Like any good parent, David Jones was terrified at what had happened. In 1992, a decade or so later, he testified that his now-adolescent kids were complaining about things like headaches or aching bones, and he wasn't sure what he should make of that. "I don't know a lot about radioactivity or how much you can, you know, take it without it having effects on you or anything. I just know she ought...she shouldn't have ate it, but it shouldn't have been there."

At the plaintiffs' table, we were hoping that an opening jolt for these all-too-human stories would keep the jurors engaged during what was becoming a long hot Mississippi summer. The enormity of what we had to do, to prove our complicated case to the jury, was exhausting just to think about. Chevron's lawyers Hortman and Martindale kept each worker from the Laurel yard on the stand for hours, politely but forcefully digging up favorable medical reports, suggesting other causes for their health problems, insisting that exposure to radioactivity at the Street properties was little above normal levels. They sympathized with the plaintiffs while gently reminding the jury that their fear of health hazards is not proof of contamination. Johnson's job was basically to be the courtroom's Nitpicker-in-Chief, and he was very, very good at what he did. The bottom line was he'd been doing radiation law for a couple of decades by then. I had been studying the topic for a little more than two years. I was always aware that if I made one small mistake, Johnson would pounce.

The exhausting reality of our task reached its high point (or low point, depending on your point of view) during the testimony of our medical expert, Dr. Callender, from Lafayette, Louisiana. Dr. Callender had examined most of the plaintiffs at our behest, in search of signs of radiation poisoning. The Louisiana physician was the linchpin of our case, since we were counting on his medical testimony not only to show the very real harm caused by Chevron's dumping of radium-226, but also to place that suffering in human terms for the jury.

Callender was able to bring home the real impact for one of the Street workers named Clifton Walker, who was just twenty-seven when the physician examined him. Walker complained of a variety of hard-to-explain ailments, including joint pain in his fingers, his knees, and even his hips, as well as inflamed sinuses and regular nosebleeds. Callender added that the patient displayed symptoms of anxiety such as a racing heartbeat and chest pain, which he did not find surprising, given the stress of learning that he'd unwittingly been exposed to cancer-causing radiation. The physician told the jury:

"Well, he seemed to be very anxious. He complained of having a...just feeling generally run-down for several years, about five years. He said he was depressed a lot, a lot of stress and worrying about the outcome of the situation. And he really didn't have any situations in his life that would bother him, that the only thing he could see was the situation at Street, Incorporated. He said he thinks that because of the stress, he has a real bad temper. He worries about dying. A lot of anxiety, depression, just kind of daydreams a lot. He feels a lot of anger and difficulty sleeping. And he stated he wasn't sure if he'd be able to continue his job because he was so preoccupied with all these thoughts and feelings, that he didn't feel like he was doing a good job at work."

It was powerful, vivid testimony, which is why Ralph Johnson and the Chevron team spent days working not only to knock it down but also to dilute its impact for the jury with ponderous and sometimes sleep-inducing cross-examination. It was having the same impact on my client, Winston Street, who'd spent five years pushing to bring this case to trial.

"He was asking him numbers that did not mean Jack-doodle-it-don't to nobody on the jury," Winston recalled years later, in his grits-and-gravy accent. "He was asking him technical questions and throwing out numbers. All he has talked about was numbers the whole time he was up there. The jury did not know—heck, I did not know—what the hell he was talking about half the time. The judge did not know what the hell he was talking [about]. He just turned them in the loops."

The scene was often punctuated by Callender punching numbers into a calculator on his watch, answering every parry that Johnson threw his way. Years later, Winston recalls those seemingly eternal weeks with a lot of cynicism.

"Oh, I will tell you what his rationale was," he told me. "He was probably billing Chevron $400 an hour. I imagine that might be his rationale, but it did not accomplish anything."

Meanwhile, our slow parade of experts was very successful, in my opinion, in showing jurors that the people who'd worked at the Street yard and who'd been exposed to these well-documented levels of radium-226 were paying an all-too-human toll. One of our best witnesses was Dr. Lisa Morrow, a University of Pittsburgh–based psychologist who was a leading authority on the mental-health effects of toxic exposure. She told the jurors that a surprisingly high percentage of the plaintiffs scored above average for post-traumatic stress disorder, or PTSD, and that on average they fared worse than soldiers coming home from the Vietnam War.

Dr. Morrow talked about interviewing workers such as Charles Gray, a machinist who had started working at the yard not long after Winston had opened it. She testified that he was taking ibuprofen daily for bone pain, and that he was terrified. "He said that he has stiffness of the joints, pain, little energy, some arthritis-type indications. He said he might have skin cancers on his nose and his forehead....He said that he has nightmares, that he often tosses in his sleep....Last year he said that he has pains all over.... 'That's my main worry, seeing people die of cancer.'"

"THE FIELD FILES" AND THE PERRY MASON MOMENT

It was powerful stuff, but it was punctuated by long stretches of monotony. As a young lawyer, taking this case to trial gave me a new appreciation for why so many complicated civil lawsuits are settled before they come within a country mile of a jury. Now that we were locked inside that Hattiesburg courtroom, the task of methodically establishing what we felt in our guts—that Chevron had poisoned the folks who worked for Winston and some of their family members—was enormous. It wasn't just a matter of hearing from the workers and then asking a doctor or a psychologist to confirm their condition, but we also had to prove that it was Chevron, among the Streets' many customers, who brought radioactive pipes to the yard.

It may have seemed pretty obvious that the oil company's pollution practices had trashed the real-estate value of the Street property, the one with the KEEP OUT—RADIATION! sign in the front yard. But establishing our case for compensatory damages required putting a local banker on the stand for two days to show what the Street property had once been worth. Sometimes we'd spend close to a whole day just going over the invoices showing which jobs came from Chevron, and which employees had worked on them, to establish their personal exposure. It was brutal, boring stuff.

But the Street brothers were determined to fight to the bitter end. They remained convinced that Chevron was still holding out, that there had to be boxes of smoking-gun "field files" somewhere that would prove that the company's oil engineers knew all about radiation at the wellhead while they were sending pipe to Street, Inc.

Looking back, you have to wonder who was the crazy one. We'd taken this thing so far that it was easy to forget who we were, that we were a young lawyer handling his first big case; a flashy-dressing, fast-talking New Orleans trial lawyer; a retired Philly cop; and a law student, using two machine-shop owners as our lead investigators. It was also easy to forget who we were up against, one of the world's wealthiest companies and its hired gun, the nation's top radiation-lawsuit attorney.

Also crazy was the snail's pace of the trial. Just one month in, it slowly dawned on all of the parties that the case, with thirty-four plaintiffs and numerous medical and radiation experts, was possibly on pace to last two years.

"That's how I have it computed so far," Judge Wingate said on July 10, 1992, referring to the pace of the trial after the first few weeks. "That if we have eighty more witnesses at the rate we've been going, I figure we'll finish around June 1994."

The quick-witted Harang snapped back: "I plan on naming my first grandchild after you because that is probably going to happen during this—and none of my daughters are even married yet."

Chevron's slow-motion strategy was very clear from the start of the trial. Part of Johnson's goal was also to convince jurors that whatever radiation came from the hot pipes that it shipped to the Streets' rattling yard wasn't so hot that it actually put the workers at an elevated health risk. From the plaintiffs' table, we thought that Johnson was using sleight of hand to minimize the amounts of radioactive dust that were in the air and on the ground. He pressed for the court to accept radiation readings that mixed the hot scale into the soil, thus diluting its impact. And a lot of his arguments were built on a bedrock of phony data and experts using questionable methodology.

But we had one thing going for us that Chevron and Ralph Johnson didn't have.

The truth.

And then one seemingly innocuous day in court very early in the trial, everything changed.

The witness on the stand was John Campbell, a former production supervisor for Chevron who had recently retired. We felt that Campbell, having worked in several oil fields in key capacities, could shed a lot of light on the inner workings of the oil giant, but at first we weren't sure we could compel him to testify. Campbell lived in Louisiana, in the New Orleans suburbs of Slidell, and the federal rule was you could only subpoena witnesses from within a 100-mile radius. We did some hasty research (no Google Maps in 1992!) and found it was ninety-two miles from Hattiesburg. Those eight miles saved our case.

Jack was questioning the witness over the steady hum of the air-conditioning. To be honest, no one was really paying close attention as Jack asked what seemed like a routine question about record keeping. Remember, with Chevron's lawyers steadfastly denying the existence of the field files at the wellhead, the implication was that better records existed somewhere else, perhaps at company headquarters.

"Mr. Campbell," Jack asked, "if you had a problem with Well X in Mississippi, and it was an emergency, how long would it take you to get the records from Dallas, Texas, or Houston, Texas, or wherever, to tell you what was in that well so you would know what type of tools to run in it?"

"I wouldn't call Houston or Dallas or nowhere," Campbell replied.

"What would you do?"

"I would go to the field files."

Heads jerked up in the courtroom. Everything seemed to stop for a moment. Jack was incredulous.

Winston says he remembers that moment like it was yesterday, and how Jack would brandish a long wooden stick when he questioned the witnesses. "He would hit himself with that stick in the hand—*pow!*," Winston recalled. "He'd say, 'Say that thing again!'"

"You would go to what?"

"I would go to the field files."

"What do you mean by the field files?"

"I would go to the file that is kept in the field on every well on that field."

I looked over at the Chevron table. The company's lawyers—Martindale, Hortman, and the hired gun Johnson—sat in shocked stone silence. Judge Wingate stared down at them from the bench. There was a long pause as the air-conditioning droned in the background like a jet plane.

I jumped and moved for Chevron to produce the records immediately, and I asked Judge Wingate to sanction the defense team for
misconduct in hiding such critical documents. Eventually, it would
be Hortman, the local Mississippi attorney, who stood up and, stam-
mering, tried to explain the oil company's inexplicable actions.
Hortman said it was all an honest misunderstanding, a matter of
confusion over the semantics.

Chevron does not maintain "field files," Hortman insisted, making
the universal air quotes gesture as the judge and our plaintiffs' table
watched in incredulity.

The company does, he noted, maintain "files in the field."

That single forty-five-second exchange on the witness stand seemed
to change everything. Judge Wingate again ordered Chevron to turn
over any and all files—"field files," "files in the field," whatever—
as soon as possible. It seems that we'd struck a gusher, to borrow
our adversaries' lingo. The next morning, we watched as a giant cart
containing six to eight large bankers' boxes of oil-field records rolled
off the elevator onto the second floor where we were trying the case.
They opened up a small conference room near the big courtroom to
store all of them, and from that morning on we worked feverishly on
two parallel tracks.

Ironically, after devoting six years of their life to getting ready
for the case, Winston and Clark had to miss a lot of the testimony,
because they spent most of each day cloistered in that small conference room, eager to finally sift through the paper trail that they considered the holy grail of their long pursuit of Chevron.

It turned out that first stacked-up cart of documents was only
the beginning of the deluge. Every day, another half-dozen boxes
were rolled into that tiny room looking out onto Main Street and the
Confederate Memorial. By the end of day one, Clark and Winston
started tagging or pulling out well tests bearing the word "radioactive" contained in boxes from the 1950s and 1960s. As we expected,

the incriminating paper trail went back for years, suggesting that Chevron had more than an inkling that its wells were producing radioactive waste as far back as four decades. We found hundreds of these documents stamped with a "field file" tracking system stamp on them, making Chevron's withholding of the paperwork look even more ridiculous.

"It's funny," Clark recalls. "A lot of those files that we had been looking for all those years, a lot of them were in one box—radioactive scale, radioactive salt. There was radioactive salt all over the place. They couldn't calibrate their gamma-ray detector on the site because it was so radioactive. They had to go off-site."

In addition, the files provided us with something else: a host of new names of Chevron engineers and employees who seemed to have awareness of the dangerous nature of the scale, based on what they'd entered in these so-called "files in the field." Most of these were new players, people we'd not had the chance to question in the initial window of pre-trial discovery. So we went back to the judge and asked him to re-open discovery, a request he had little choice but to approve, given the tidal wave of new, damning evidence. The problem, of course, was that this new flurry of depositions would have to take place while we were still building our case inside that Hattiesburg courtroom for forty hours a week. To prove that Chevron was willfully and wantonly negligent in polluting the Streets' property and contaminating the workers there, we would need to work around the clock, tracking down retired Chevron engineers on the weekends.

Still, these depositions were a boon to our case. In early November, I sat down with Chevron's lawyers to depose one of the new, critical company employees that we'd identified—a then-fifty-eight-year-old recent retiree named Luke Halpain, who'd been a longtime drilling engineer and supervisor. At first, Halpain stuck to the company line, that no one was aware of radioactive scale before early 1986, right before the unannounced visit to the Street yard. But now I was able to hammer him, with report after report from the field files we'd now located going back to the late 1960s and early 1970s, in which field engineers had noted high radiation readings. For example, one field file from September 1971 indicated radioactivity in the production pipes.

"[S]omebody should have been aware," Halpain conceded. "I mean, it's typed right on the log."

"Well, someone was aware, weren't they, sir?" I asked.

"Yes."

"Because they don't throw these in a garbage can, do they?"

"No."

COMING TO BLOWS

Midway through the trial, the stress was starting to get to me. I should have been buoyed by the revelation of the field files, which made it more likely that our efforts would lead to a large payday, either through a jury verdict or at least by a more lucrative deal than what Chevron had been offering to the Streets and their workers so far. But that felt like a faraway fantasy. The reality was that I was now a thirty-two-year-old lawyer more than five years out of law school, and I was flat broke. My arrangement with Jack meant that I got paid when we won or settled a case, and the months that I'd spent in Hattiesburg had shut off the income spigot all together. Jack had taught me to live by the code of "eat what we kill," but every day that we sat in Judge Wingate's courtroom was a day that we didn't "kill" anything. That payout from the auto wreck that provided Barry and me with a short burst of prosperity was completely evaporated, too.

I was worried that Barry, who was still a student, and I were going to get kicked out of our little apartment in Metairie, and there was the prospect of losing the used Porsche. I worked harder than ever—sometimes sixteen or eighteen hours a day—reviewing testimony or preparing for the next day's witness until midnight, waking up at the crack of dawn to keep going. I tend to be forward-looking and confident—too cocky for my own good, some would say—but doubt was creeping in. Had it all been a reckless mistake, taking that phone call from Winston and taking his case? I'd rolled the dice, in the Smith family tradition, but what if it came up snake eyes, like it so often had for my dad?

I began to pin my hope of paying the immediate and growing stack of bills on a couple of older matters that had worked their way through the pipeline, including one large case that Jack and I had worked together. Several times during our long Hattiesburg nights, I asked Jack about the money and he insisted that the defendant was slow in paying. Happens all the time, he said.

The good thing about being young was that it didn't take a whole lot to take my mind off my troubles. When I look back through the fog of time at those Hattiesburg nights, my best memories are of the times we veered off Highway 49 on the way home from the courthouse into the gravel parking lot of a road-house called Donanelle's Bar and Grill, a little log cabin nestled up dark against the piney woods with a sign on the top boasting You Can't Beat Our Meat. Open the door and, if you've never spent time in Mississippi, you'll find the kind of place you probably once thought only existed in a movie, wallpapered with dollar bills marked up with well wishes from customers, butcher paper on the tables, and a heart-attack-size stick of butter in every baked potato. The neckties of unprepared, over-attired businessmen had all been cut off, and were hanging from the ceiling. I can still taste the hotness of those ribs a couple of decades later. A couple of their Arctic-cold beers from the cooler and you could forget that somewhere back in town, Johnson was reviewing the trial transcripts on the front porch of his quiet B and B, abstaining from Coca-Cola.

But in reality, those neon-backlit nights at Donanelle's were too rare. There was too much work to stay ahead of Chevron's top-dollar lawyers, especially with all the new evidence that was pouring in. The pressure of so many nights cooped up in that cottage deep in the dark Mississippi night, and our ongoing worries that we were somehow being listened to, began to eat away at us. Jack had been a wonderful mentor who introduced me to the dog-eat-dog ways of the successful trial lawyer, but he was starting to get on my nerves. I'm a morning person by nature, and sometimes I was even getting up in the middle of the night to study up, to try to compete with Johnson on his knowledgeable terms. But then, it was an autumn of discovery on a lot of fronts. I continued to press Jack about the money from the unrelated case. Back home in Metairie, my landlord was starting to slide eviction notices under my door. One day, in the depths of my worries over money, I walked into the federal courthouse in Hattiesburg and ran into one of the lawyers from the case over in Columbia, Mississippi, that had been settled earlier in the year. "What happened to the money?" I asked.

"What do you mean?" he replied. "We paid that money to Jack two months ago."

One night after a few of us had stopped off for dinner, I collapsed on the sofa in the main living room. Deep in REM sleep, I suddenly jerked up with a sharp sudden jolt—someone had stuck an ice cube down my back in the middle of the night. I looked up in the purple haze of slumber and there was Jack standing over me, laughing manically. I'm not sure how he thought I was going to react. Maybe the unprovoked ice assault reminded me of those days when I'd been bullied in high school for being different or when I was occasionally woken up by two boisterous little brothers in the middle of the night. Everyone in my family knew never to wake me up in deep sleep because I always came up swinging.

So I unleashed a torrent of words that would have made a sailor blush and came up with my fists. My anger about finding out that Jack had lied to me about the money after he knew I had gotten an eviction notice was more than I could handle. He did not realize how pissed off I really was. I punched him in the mouth and immediately realized that it was a stupid move to hit a trial lawyer in the mouth in the middle of a trial. I should have gut punched him. Jack was super pissed off and started coming back at me.

His attitude changed slightly when I yelled, "That's for stealing my Columbia money and lying about it." He realized his anger could never come close to matching mine at that point. He hesitated for a second from the verbal assault, giving Ron enough time to step between us. It could have been a disaster. I was much bigger than Jack and he was fifteen years older than me but he had been a successful amateur boxer with a killer left. We would likely have really hurt each other and disrupted the trial. Jack ended up with a bloodied and slightly swollen lip. That was all.

Then I gathered my stuff and took it back to the spare room out behind the cottage and announced that as I could no longer work with Jack, I was quitting the case. I was that livid. This, after I had thrown so much of myself into it. It was Clark who sat me down and talked me out of that. After having lost so many other lawyers before I showed up, there was no way the Streets could start over again, not when we were on the same wavelength on how to win the case. I did resolve once and for all to quit working with Jack as soon as the case was over, but how would I ever make it through so many more weeks in Hattiesburg? Christmas was fast approaching, and we hadn't even rested our case.

Meanwhile, more boxes of Chevron's once-nonexistent field files continued to show up. As the trial dragged on, less of our time in court was spent on the complicated medical testimony and more of it was spent voicing our frustration over what we argued was withholding of basic evidence. "It just seems odd, Your Honor, in this case, whenever the plaintiffs need crucial evidence, it disappears," I had told Judge Wingate during one of these battles back in August.

I could see that we were winning Wingate over. After many weeks of frustration, he demanded an opportunity to visit the main site where these files were being kept—the Chevron headquarters for its major Mississippi drilling operation, located in Baxterville field—so that he could get a better handle on what was going on. This was a critical moment, because a finding by Wingate that the oil company or its lawyers had committed discovery abuse would swing the overall case in our favor.

I will never forget the moment that our party opened the door and we entered the large room where Chevron had been keeping the records, and keeping them from us. It was a long room stacked high with metal filing cabinets that were filled to the brim with the now infamous field files. The same files that Chevron was ordered on multiple occasions to produce by the judge years prior. It was remarkable to finally see it in person, and after photographing the scene, I looked over at the judge. He didn't say a word, but he appeared stunned.

"He called for the in-camera inspection of the office down in Baxterville and they probably had a building fifty foot long so they had—I do not know how many wells they got in that field, probably a thousand," Winston recalled. "And they had a building there, probably fifty feet long with filing cabinets just full of well files."

An unemotional man, Judge Wingate had to be thinking if he should declare a mistrial, after the court and the jurors had devoted so many months to the case. I can't even imagine what was going through the minds of the Chevron legal team at that instant. A mistrial that was their fault would have required Chevron to pay our costs, such as attorney and expert witness fees along with substantial sanctions. But Wingate reserved judgment in the matter—in essence, putting Chevron on probation while he mulled over the bombshells that had gone off in his chambers that fall.

Inside the courtroom, everyone was getting testy. Winston Street recalled that I was losing my naturally thin patience, and he was probably right. "Stuart would get up there and argue with the judge, that's what teed the judge off," he later recalled in a conversation. "Stuart just wouldn't shut up. If he had a point to make, he'd get up there and make it and the judge would be hollering and waving his arms and Stuart would just keep on yakking."

As hard as the ordeal was for the attorneys, I can only imagine what was going through the minds of the jurors. These were just salt-of-the-earth citizens of Mississippi who came home from work one night and found a letter in their mailbox asking them to report for jury duty, and now their lives had been turned upside down for months.

"That case was a hardship on a lot of them poor folks on that jury," Winston recalled later. "We had one girl who had a baby. I mean, she was not even showing when the case started and she had to take leave to have the baby before it was over." Even as we crept up on the six-month anniversary, Judge Wingate's doomsday prediction that the case could last yet another eighteen months loomed like a nightmare in the back of everyone's brain. As plaintiffs' attorneys, we had to worry about what effect the days of sometimes soul-crushing testimony would have on the jurors once they got inside a locked room to deliberate. Would they take it out on us?

At this stage, we had the liability and punitive case locked up. We had the mistrial for discovery abuse in our back pocket. The judge would likely inform the jurors of the field-file fiasco if we did not ask for the mistrial. All that was left was for us to prove our case that Chevron also lied about how concentrated and dangerous the radium scale really was.

The straw that broke the camel's back was discovered by an unlikely source—another member of our own low-budget "dream team," the law student and clerk who was staying with us, James Cox. During the oil boom years of the 1980s, Cox had started a career as a petroleum engineer for Schlumberger in Louisiana before he shifted gears and enrolled in law school. Even though he was now primarily a student of the law, his knowledge of how the oil industry worked was invaluable in the Chevron case. Cox was still an active member of SPE (the Society of Petroleum Engineers). One day in the middle of the trial, he was going through a stack of the newsletters that he still regularly received as an SPE member. He was flipping through an issue from 1991—i.e., the year before the trial started— when he saw a notice for an oil and gas environmental conference in the Netherlands. One of the presenters at the conference was none other than Henry T. Miller; the blurb noted that he would be delivering not one but two separate papers on the risks of TERM.

Cox said he didn't recall seeing the TERM papers in the paltry amount of documents that Chevron had produced when we had asked for any documents from Miller related to TERM during the discovery process. In fact, Chevron had been ordered to produce all such documents years ago. Based on the discrepancy, Judge Wingate ordered that Miller (who, coincidentally or not, had retired from Chevron six months earlier) be made available for a deposition. It would be our first real crack at the oil industry's top radiation expert, because he had initially been deposed by one of the Streets' initial, long-ago-dismissed attorneys.

It turned out that Miller had taken a new job up in Paducah, Kentucky, advising a nuclear power plant there on radiation safety. With Wingate's OK, we agreed that Miller would be deposed in Kentucky while the trial was in recess. Frankly, it was a relief to get out of Hattiesburg for a day or two, even if it was to go to Paducah. We arrived in the afternoon; Johnson presumably went off to meet with his client, now the star witness on which everything seemed to turn. I headed off to my small room in a motel on the main strip. I was about to hit the bar downstairs for a quick nightcap when the phone rang in my hotel. I looked over at the phone. It was 9 o' clock.

Ralph Johnson was on the line.

"I need to see you. Tonight."

My heart raced. There was a sense of urgency in Johnson's normally flat and plaintive Utah-rooted, Spock-like voice that I had never heard before.

About ten minutes later, Johnson knocked on my hotel room door. He seemed agitated. And he was carrying a stack of flagged documents, probably about two feet high. They had never been produced before.

"I'm sorry," Johnson said. He mumbled something about how he had not been involved in the case the first time that Miller was deposed and was not involved in the document production in response to the court's previous order, which was true. It appeared he knew Chevron was in big trouble and he was not going to take the fall. He had seen the papers for the first time, just as I was about to. As I looked at the thick stack, I noticed that a number of the documents had yellow Post-it notes attached.

"I went through them before I came over," he said. "I wanted to flag the ones I thought you'd most be interested in." He did not look very happy—although to be honest he never looked happy. A moment later, he was gone.

I called room service. It was going to be a long night. I went straight to the flagged materials. The first one was those papers that Miller had presented in Holland, the one that James Cox had found the announcement for. In it, the expert discussed how dangerous that pipe cleaning could be without the right protective clothing. It turned out the documents showed that Chevron, which had feigned shock and surprise at the discovery of radium-226 in the Mississippi oil fields in 1986, had actually carried out extensive studies and concluded there was a real risk to workers of overexposure. The documents directly contradicted many of the assumptions Chevron's experts had made in defending the case.

That wasn't all. There were documents in the stack pertaining directly to the contamination of the Streets' property, including one that recorded a finding of radioactivity in the dust at the site that was much higher than the highest reading that Chevron's lawyers had produced before. Chevron's experts were assuming the scale was only a few hundred times background levels while the Miller test result was 6,200 times higher than background. Chevron had failed to disclose test results from my own client's property for six years! Throughout the trial, Johnson had been arguing that the real number should be much lower, claiming that the radioactive scale was mixed in with the soil and thus diluted. But Miller's papers that had not been turned over to us showed that the evidence in the courtroom, which we'd been dancing around for months in front of the judge and jury, was not truly representative of the site when Miller first arrived there.

I could not believe what I was reading. I'd long suspected, practically from the day that I met the Streets three years earlier, that Chevron was holding back, but now I was shocked to see both the boldness and the extent of the most highly relevant but previously undisclosed evidence splayed across the bed of a Kentucky motel. This material was a significant part of the evidence we submitted to the judge in support of our motion for sanctions and a mistrial.

The next morning, I had my chance to finally question H.T. Miller. But now the main thing I wanted to ask was why had he and Chevron's lawyers not produced the documents? But he told me that he had turned over all the papers he had, to Chevron's in-house lawyers. The reality was becoming clear. The information that Chevron had known for years about the dangers of scale and had attempted to hide the full extent of the contamination of the Streets' yard was incredibly damning, but the issue of discovery abuse, which I intended to argue in Judge Wingate's courtroom, was going to be the last nail in Chevron's coffin.

When we returned to Hattiesburg, it felt like the final doomed moves of a chess match already to the point of checkmate. When Judge Wingate learned of what had happened in Kentucky that weekend, he spoke from the bench with anger and bewilderment, while there was mostly chastened silence from the defense table. "I don't need to tell you what I am going to do if I find discovery abuse," he said, gazing at the trio of Johnson, Martindale, and Hortman before dismissing the courtroom out into the dark and chilly December night. I think the lawyers all knew that a finding of discovery abuse and contempt of court by Chevron was likely a foregone conclusion.

It was a short time later that Johnson got on the phone again. This time he called Jack. Chevron, it seemed, was finally ready to pay. I have to say that was one of the happiest nights of my life.

It only took a few days to wrap things up. As is often the case in these matters, the deal barred us from publicly disclosing the terms, even to this day. Suffice it to say, we were finally in the driver's seat. At the end, we received an offer that was acceptable to Winston and Clark, and we were able to bring some economic solace to the workers there who'd been thrown out of a job after risking their good health cleaning out Chevron's pipes.

There was one more thing that Ralph Johnson still needed to know, and that was what on earth was in that box? So Jack opened it to reveal a CAUTION—RADIOACTIVE MATERIAL sticker, which we contended the regulations required to be affixed to each pipe. One of our main theories of liability had been that it was a violation of the Mississippi state regulations, which required warnings on sources of radiation such as the pipe. We'll never know if it would have had the desired effect on the jury.

One one hand, there was a part of me that never understood why Chevron had fought this thing so hard for so long. It was clear from day one that they were liable for something. There was no doubt that they'd sent highly radioactive pipe to the Streets' pipe yard; the only question was whether they knew what they were doing a little bit or they knew what they were doing a lot.

On the other hand, part of me understood exactly why they fought. We were looking to establish a brand-new area of environmental law, one that could gain a small measure of justice for workers and other citizens who'd been poisoned all across the oil patch of the Deep South, and could cost Big Oil hundreds of millions of dollars. What's more, the big picture really became much clearer for me. I had come of age during an oil boom in southern Louisiana, when a surge in off-shore drilling had been a source of jobs during a national recession and millions of dollars in tax revenue that had filled the state coffers. But the Streets showed me a different side of the Big Oil behemoth, a system that valued profits over people, that didn't care who got caught in the process, and that was perfectly content to try to cover its tracks if necessary. It is our job as trial lawyers to try to make the costs of doing good less than the costs of doing bad.

I had also learned that there are some decent and hardworking public servants who care about the environment out there, people like Mississippi's radiation expert Eddie Fuente. But their good work tends to get buried in the stench of power politics, and by their bosses who are beholden to campaign checks from the oil executives and their millionaire pals. The Streets and their employees had been chasing after justice for six long years, and in the end, the only place they could find it was inside a courtroom with a fair and impartial judge, and where the rules of evidence finally applied. Civil action could be a form of crude justice at times, but it was the only way, sometimes, to get any justice at all when the oil companies and their billions were involved.

When I hopped into that old Porsche and zoomed down I-59 with Hattiesburg, the cottage by the lake, and Donanelle's spicy ribs in my rearview mirror for the last time, I was a free man. I was about to be minus a law firm, but I had no doubt what I wanted to do with my career. Learning the ins and outs of radiological health was kind of like learning brain surgery, and now I was ready to operate.

This was my life now—I was going to war with Big Oil. And Big Oil was going to fight back with everything it had.

BOOK
TWO

THE EMPIRE STRIKES BACK

ONE MORNING IN 1986, an employee of Chevron named John Franks grabbed two empty plastic jugs, hopped in his car, and started driving east, across the shimmering green marshes of America's Gulf Coast, on a top secret mission. Once he reached Hammond, Louisiana, Franks departed the swampy environs of I-10 and headed north into southern Mississippi, across a landscape of steep hills and spectacular longleaf yellow pines. His destination was the small outpost of Brookhaven, once the heart of the Mississippi oil patch, where as many as 100 wells once pumped nearly every available drop of crude from the ground, littering the hidden backwoods with rusty piles of pipe and large gravel pits of thick, noxious sludge.

It took nearly six hours for Franks to reach his destination, which was a small mom-and-pop gas station and country store called the Case Grocery, several miles off the interstate. Its small, sunbaked gravel parking lot was carved out of a thick stand of Southern pines, and there was a cluttered, humming machine shop around the side road. He took the two jugs out of the car and—without introducing himself—asked at the counter if it would be OK to fill them up with water. His mission accomplished, Franks jumped back in the car, turned around and drove six hours back home.

Back in Chevron's laboratory in Houston, chemists tested the water to confirm what employees of the oil giant had already secretly suspected, that the water that business owner James Case—and his family, and his neighbors who lived in the oil field—were drinking and showering in every day was polluted with unsafe levels of radium-226, lead, arsenic, chromium, and a host of other toxic compounds. The pollution was the inevitable result of decades of carelessness by an icon of Big Oil that treated a rural Mississippi community like a giant toilet bowl. A 1996 report by the U.S. Geological Survey found that massive oil-field production in the vicinity of Brookhaven had significantly contaminated just over half of the 177 wells it examined over a broad area. It turned out there was a long trail of evidence tending to show that Chevron had known for years that it was poisoning the water underneath the Brookhaven oil field, and that it chose to do nothing.

It was not long after news of the settlement in the Street case that I discussed a potential Case family pipe yard suit against Chevron with the family's lawyer, James Kitchens (now a Mississippi Supreme Court justice), who asked me to join him in their legal battle against Chevron. The environmental degradation we found in Brookhaven confirmed a suspicion that had first originated during our initial fight, that what had taken place in Laurel and at Winston Street's yard was not an isolated incident, but a warning sign of widespread radioactive pollution that existed across the Gulf oil patch. Throughout the 1990s, these small towns—off the beaten path, their names unknown to most Americans—became the burning heart of a war that pitted Big Oil companies against regular folks who were the victims of systematic, unchecked pollution. It was fought in legislative chambers, in bureaucratic back offices, and inside courtrooms, and I was on the front line.

I was still a young lawyer in early 1993, but I was riding an understandable surge of optimism after we'd gotten the better of Chevron in Judge Wingate's Hattiesburg courtroom. In January of that year, Bill Clinton took over the Oval Office to end a dozen years of pro-business Republican rule, and it was hard not to believe that a more active government would penalize the polluters and finally mandate real cleanups, aiding my goal of achieving justice for the property owners who'd been harmed. Simply put, the Street case had opened up an entirely new field of environmental case law, and the strategy now was to pursue justice in the Brookhavens of America.

In some ways, the Case situation was like the Street case on steroids. Certainly, there were similarities: Chevron, again, was a major customer, and once again state official Eddie Fuente and the EPA played a critical role in uncovering the radioactivity on the site. But unlike Winston Street, the Cases' pipe-rattling yard had been in business for decades, a much longer period, which meant that the property was that much more contaminated and the family was, in theory, entitled to more damages. The Cases actually lived out behind the pipe-rattling yard and the gas station, and their kids had frolicked in the radioactive dust. The exposure hadn't just been for a longer period of time, the family had literally been living in a radioactive shadow for years.

Indeed, further investigation revealed that the extent of pollution was far greater than what we had encountered in Laurel. Investigators from the EPA, on their one visit to Mississippi at Fuente's request, found radium-226 in the grass in the Case cow pasture at levels 160 times above background proving once and for all that the poisonous radioactive material from the pipe scale will leach out and enter the food chain. There was so much contamination that it was migrating away from the Case property into the surrounding community; our research revealed that some of the poisonous radium was washed into a drainage ditch and showed that traces had washed as far as a half-mile away.

Although we had been fumbling in the dark, at times, during the Street case, our legal efforts on behalf of the Case family had the advantage of building on everything we'd learned about radiological contamination in Laurel, things that we'd learned from top scientific experts. We were also aided again by our self-taught private eyes, Winston and Clark. We analyzed data from the EPA's site visit to extrapolate that a worker exposed to the radioactive scale at the Case yard was bombarded with 7.3 rems of radiation per year, well above the federal occupational and Mississippi safety standards and elevating the cancer risk to about 200 times greater than what experts typically deemed acceptable.

Dr. Stan Waligora and Rick Haaker, who are two of the nation's leading radiation protection consultants, along with Marvin Resnikoff, an authority on radioactive waste disposal, all worked with us in Brookhaven to develop a state-of-the-art dose model that is still used today. At the Case property, Waligora said this new model showed "that these people were grievously overexposed."

What's more, our investigation into oil production and waste disposal in and around Brookhaven revealed something else that was arguably more troubling: a widespread pattern of highly unsafe dumping in which Big Oil companies, knowing full well the risks yet allowing local citizens to remain in the dark, littered these poor, rural communities with toxic and radioactive wastes, frequently in ways that contaminated the local drinking water supply. This decades-long environmental abuse that typically targeted poor and working-class communities was shocking in its callousness, and yet we found these patterns were repeated across the American South. While we were working on the Case litigation, the other neighbors who did not clean pipe began to contact us about water pollution. We discovered dozens of unlined pits with radioactive hazardous waste just sitting in the open and many dozens of rotten wells that had not been properly maintained and were leaking due to lack of integrity. When Chevron fracked the Brookhaven field using waterflooding techniques, we filed a lawsuit based on good evidence claiming the pollutants seeped into and damaged one of the largest fresh water aquifers in the entire United States.

In the Brookhaven matter, our expert Dr. Waligora—who had once worked as a radiation safety consultant for Exxon—said in terms that were crude but impossible to dispute that "the oil companies defecated on these people and treated them like serfs." It was in connection with defending Chevron in Brookhaven that Martindale, who was still around despite the Street debacle, expressed shock that these people would sue, because "Chevron put shoes on their feet." It's hard to believe that such a thing could happen in a wealthy and caring democracy like the United States of America, but it happened again and again and again. In my career I have never seen an oil company encounter a corner it did not want to cut if it could and would make them more money. That is the sad legacy of the industry.

The oil field around Brookhaven had started booming in the 1940s when oil companies raced in to lease these resource-rich lands at bargain-basement prices, sometimes as low as twenty-five cents an acre. In return, the oil firms—and in Brookhaven, it was Chevron's predecessors that gained control of most of these leases—made what was supposed to be a legally-binding promise not to pollute the leaseholder's land. This was a promise that energy giants had no intention of keeping. Even in a pro-business state like Mississippi, officials passed legislation and enacted regulations in the 1940s aimed at forcing the oil companies to properly dispose of their waste, and with good reason. The Brookhaven oil patch sits atop the Southern Hills Regional Aquifer, which was once a pristine source of drinking water for thousands of people from Baton Rouge up to Jackson, Mississippi. As far back as 1947, Mississippi, which is not a state known for commitment to environmentalism, enacted some tough standards against pollution because of mounting concern from rural sportsmen that the oil companies were polluting their local streams.

Indeed, with little fanfare, in the 1950s, 1960s, and 1970s, state and federal laws were enacted about disposal of radium-226 or wastewater, culminating in the federal Clean Water Act and the Safe Drinking Water Act, a law that Chevron violated repeatedly through its failure to maintain the integrity of its waterflood injection wells. The message to companies like Chevron was supposed to be clear: Any radioactive or toxic drilling wastes should be injected deep underground, below the aquifer. And any storage pits or reservoirs should be lined to prevent any poisons from leaching into the water supply and immediately cleaned up and closed when they were no longer needed. Oil wells should not only be well maintained to prevent leaks, but also capped at the end of their useful production.

WATER ON FIRE

My battle finally came to a head in a place called Martha, Kentucky.

In 1993, I was asked to visit this small, off-the-beaten-path rural enclave in eastern Kentucky. An environmental activist in the Bluegrass State had heard about the Street case and asked if I could help out some landowners in a small oil-producing corridor near the West Virginia border who were trying, with little success, to get

Ashland Oil (the maker of top-selling Valvoline motor oil) to clean up their properties now laced with radiation.

Nothing in my experience along the Gulf Coast had prepared me for the ecological destruction that I found when I finally visited Martha, an unincorporated area with roughly 250 families scattered across lush, beautiful rolling hills and meadows. Ashland Oil was long gone from Martha; the company, like Chevron in Brookhaven, had used the isolated community as a testing ground for what essentially was a precursor to the twenty-first-century fracking boom. They injected massive quantities of water under the earth to extract millions of barrels of crude oil, peaking in the 1970s when world oil prices were at historical highs. By 1988, however, Ashland had mostly abandoned these hillsides in the face of pressure from the federal EPA over its dumping of hazardous sludge and other environmental practices. (If Ronald Reagan's toothless EPA came down on a polluter, that's a sure sign they were doing something really, really bad!)

But Martha, Kentucky, had been deeply scarred by its brief love affair with Big Oil. Nowadays, wells plugged with nothing more than tree stumps dot the once-bustling landscape, abandoned roadbeds lead to nowhere, heaps of rusting twisted oil pipe are piled high, and old brine holding ponds and discharge pits rest along the hillsides like shallow graves. The creeks are still clogged with oil slicks, the messy aftermath of Ashland's practice of using too much water pressure to extract every last drop of oil from the ground.

What the residents had, of course, not been told during the boom years of the 1970s and 1980s, and what we later learned in the course of discovery in a lawsuit, is that the oil that Ashland had forced out with its deep-water injection was heavily contaminated by radium-226 and other toxic oil-field waste, which is prevalent in the Devonian shale there. After the briny and radioactive wastewater was separated from the crude oil, we learned it was dumped in sludge pits or even disposed of in a local body of water, Blaine Creek. The worst part, however, was the poison that the people of Martha could not even see or smell. As it happened again and again in the South in the 1980s at the end of that era's oil boom, the radioactive contamination was only discovered by accident. In 1988, a load of pipe was sent to a scrapyard near Martha and set off a radiation detector. This launched the investigation that soon required my attention.

When I came to Martha five years later, the first person I met was a successful local businessman named Victor Ferguson, who'd bought a large piece of farmland outside of Martha and built a new home on the rolling hillside. I took out my radiation detectors and walked across his property and was dismayed to find that practically every inch showed evidence of contamination. In the stream near his house, you could poke the muddy bottom with a stick and an oil sheen would appear. Next was Bill Mullins, a native who owned a twenty-five-acre property and whose family had worked for Ashland dating back to 1953. Like his neighbor Ferguson, Mullins had built a new home on the parcel, only to be told by a Kentucky state regulator that it was now too dangerous to live in because of the radiation levels. Most of the worst contamination on Mullins's land took place during Ashland's hasty retreat in the late 1980s, as work crews ripped out oil pipelines and scattered radioactive scale all over his parcel of land. When I met Mullins, he shared the frustration of many Martha residents, in that Ashland had carried out a so-called "cleanup" of his property that residents felt was so grossly inadequate.

Mullins recounts how he and the local radiation officer once took a water sample from the faucet of a resident's home—and lit it on fire. "We turned on the tap and filled up a glass," he recalls. "You could smell the oil in it. We put a lighter to the water just to see what would happen, and it just burned blue." (This, I should note, was more than two decades before the Josh Fox documentary, Oscar-nominated *Gasland*, alerted millions of Americans to the joys of being able to light your tap water on fire, courtesy of the oil and gas industry.)

There was one other vitally important fact that emerged during our investigation of Martha. We learned that the true extent of the oil industry's knowledge about TERM ran much deeper than we had realized when we'd been carrying out our discovery in the Street case back in Mississippi. Once again, H.T. Miller and the Big Oil lobbying group, the API, were right in the middle of it. It turned out that Ashland's medical director, Dr. Earl Arp, had sent a memo to his supervisors warning them of the dangers of environmental pollution from oil-field radioactive material. The letter was dated November 21, 1982.

But here's the kicker: Arp's urgent letter (which of course, as far as anyone could tell, was never acted on by his higher-ups) was based on a presentation to the API prepared by H.T. Miller, and he even attached Miller's comprehensive, thirty-one-page report on TERM to his letter. Miller's paper not only discussed the health hazards of radioactive oil waste, but also spelled out in clear terms the massive costs to the oil industry if TERM were regulated as a hazardous waste, providing an easy motive for a cover-up. Miller's API report proved that oil companies had exposed workers and neighbors to radioactivity for at least four years before taking action, and as such, became a kind of Rosetta Stone in our larger probe of Big Oil. It seemed as though what they were trying to avoid was so bad, it was worth it to them not to cede an inch, and to keep acknowledging (and paying) as little as possible to the people they'd treated so poorly.

Even when faced with Judge Wingate's wrath and contempt of court, Chevron never produced this smoking gun. If it existed, we were going to have to get it from another oil company. It was a beautiful irony and because of all the documents I got from so many different companies, I now knew far more about their TERM issues than they or their lawyers did.

But the most frustrating thing about the environmental havoc that was wreaked on Martha was not so much Ashland's predictable resistance to cleaning up its mess, but, as in Brookhaven, that their outrageous behavior was largely tolerated by state and federal officials. This was an era in which the oil companies fought tooth-and-nail against any regulation of its poisonous wastes. It had not been long since the gas lines and price shocks of the Arab oil-embargo years, and so lobbyists persuaded lawmakers and politically appointed regulators that expensive, safe-disposal rules would cripple domestic drilling and that the industry should be allowed to self-regulate.

In Martha, Ashland Oil dragged its feet for years before carrying out any type of remediation at the contaminated properties. When it finally performed some cleanup work under a 1993 agreement, residents believed the work was both inadequate and haphazard, leaving behind piles of old radioactive pipe or pits of unsightly sludge, which all left their rich Kentucky soil laced with unhealthy levels of that silent, deadly killer, radium-226. Echoing battles that were taking place in state capitals across the South, Ashland legally fought off proposals that would have treated the wastes from its toxic sludge pits, the tons of tainted soil, and miles of hot, contaminated pipes with the same strict rules as the radioactive by-products of a nuclear power plant or uranium mine. Instead, incredibly, Ashland won approval to take the radiation-laced wastes to what it farcically called a "temporary" landfill, an abandoned surface mine in the neighboring community of Catlettsburg where 115,000 tons of this radioactive waste had been piled, which they covered with only a plastic tarp! This "temporary disposal site" remains in the Martha community to this day.

But the emotional wounds that Ashland Oil left behind in Martha are even more painful than the physical damage. Years after the discovery of those hot pipes triggered the crisis, residents gathered weekly in a local church to share their complaints and to press state officials for more aggressive action. Most of the land they own is unsellable now, which makes it worthless. They talked in hushed tones about neighbors diagnosed with cancer—an astonishing 176 out of 600 residents have died in recent years—and pressed for answers on whether or not Ashland's radioactive gunk is the cause. The holy grail of their quest is a cat that was born a few years back on a contaminated property with six feet, two tails, and two heads. The freakish creature is preserved in formaldehyde and shown to new visitors as a symbol of the fear that still permeates Martha, Kentucky.

Ashland, like Chevron before it, began putting up a fight, even hiring Ralph Johnson, the slick lawyer Chevron used to attempt to beat us in the Laurel case. But Ashland finally decided to settle after one particular heated hearing in front of the local state court judge, one which I will never forget. I was arguing that Ashland should give us access to the entire oil field to test for radiation levels. Ashland was very opposed to this and Ralph Johnson jumped up and started to speak before I was finished. The judge stopped him cold and asked, "Who are you?" Johnson told him his name, and when asked where he was from, he replied, "Washington, D.C."

The judge then said, "Mr. Johnson, you will not speak in my courtroom until you are spoken to." I could tell right away that Johnson did not want to hang out with this judge for longer than it took to settle the case. The clients received generous settlements and a promise from Ashland to clean up the oil field, as required by Ashland's agreement with the state of Louisiana. As of several years ago, the cleanup was still not completed to the satisfaction of residents as a direct result of the state of Kentucky's refusal to require Ashland to live up to its promises.

What happened in Martha was a microcosm of the fifteen years after the TERM issue went public in the mid-1980s. Chevron's settlement in the Street case in Mississippi had opened a brand-new avenue of justice against Big Oil, but rather than change their evil ways, the oil giants threw all their clout at shutting that avenue down.

They were maddeningly successful, nowhere more so than in my home state of Louisiana.

TAKING ON THE OIL REPUBLIC OF LOUISIANA

In 1993, I met for the first time a young, soft-spoken public servant in Baton Rouge named Richard Brackin. The story he told me was a remarkable one.

It begins around Christmastime in 1985, a few months before the discovery of radioactivity at the Streets' property in neighboring Mississippi. He'd only been hired a month earlier by the Louisiana DEQ in what was then known as its Nuclear Energy Division. Brackin was a radiological safety officer; there are three nuclear power plants either located in or just bordering Louisiana, and his job mostly involved training small-town first responders on how to protect citizens in the event of an emergency at one of these facilities.

But like a lot of folks who got involved in the TERM issue in the 1980s and 1990s, Brackin's life was turned upside down by one phone call.

In December 1985, a disgruntled employee of a well-logging company—a firm that specialized in mapping the geology underground—contacted the DEQ as a whistleblower. He claimed that a small metal device known as a radioactive source, a kind of well-logging device used in the oil exploration process had been tossed carelessly in the woods around Lake Charles in the southwestern corner of the state. His call prompted an extensive search for the device, which itself was highly radioactive, and the young public-health agent Brackin was asked to drive to the Lake Charles area with a radiation detector on his dashboard in hopes of pinpointing the source.

"I was on the west side of Lake Charles—I went to the back of (an industrial) plant and started to get high readings around a pond,"

Brackin recalled to me years later. "This was kind of a wooded area so I got out of the truck, and as I got closer to the water, the meter basically went off the scale."

The radioactive source was nowhere to be found, but Brackin decided to collect a sample of water from the pond and bring it back to the lab for additional analysis based on the readings he was getting. But the testing showed that the water itself did not have an abnormally high level of radiation. A coworker in the department explained to Brackin that the problem was more likely that radium from water produced from oil drilling was dumped into that pond, and the radioactive material had settled on the bottom, where it would migrate gradually into the water table.

It was an alarming discovery, but it was just the beginning. Remember, the mid-1980s marked the final years of an oil-drilling boom across the American Sunbelt, as the big energy companies raced to find cheaper domestic sources of fuel in the face of two devastating Arab oil embargoes. Around 1985, world prices collapsed and oil exploration in the South began to sharply decline, but the environmental damage had already been done. The Lake Charles incident was merely the first of a series of shocking finds involving oil, improper dumping, and radioactivity.

"I recall that in Lafayette they had supply trucks that were somewhere in a pasture where they were being cleaned or worked on," Brackin said. "They carried response equipment, including radiation meters. Well, somebody turned his meter on, and they started getting a reading, and they called us to check it out. It turned out to be a place where they cleaned production pipe. This, we thought, was a problem. There were a lot of remote areas that were being used for that. There wasn't always a facility, a lot of pipe cleaning was just done out in a field, without any regard to radioactive materials."

By now, Brackin's initial task of training cops and firefighters was taking a backseat; instead, he was tackling the TERM crisis full-time, and within a short time, he became the point man for the DEQ in dealing with radioactive waste in the oil patch. The existing state guidelines were very stringent for dealing with radioactive material. The problem was that the oil companies wanted their own special, less-stringent set of regulations, and now Brackin was on the brink of doing something that the Reagan administration in Washington seemed unwilling to do—craft strict, cradle-to-grave regulations for the disposal of TERM. This effort—which would have required Big Oil to spend hundreds of millions of dollars to keep the environment clean—was underway at the same time as the Street trial in Mississippi, so the stakes for the industry were huge. The attacks were rising on all sides as their shoddy practices finally came back to haunt them.

It also bumped Brackin into an arena that he desperately wanted to avoid: politics. He was about to learn that in politics, like everywhere else, timing is everything. For much of the twentieth century, Big Oil was king in Louisiana, much like cotton had been in the nineteenth century. Indeed, the state's first major oil well was drilled in 1901, just months after the famous Spindletop gusher in neighboring Texas; Big Oil expanded again in the 1930s with the first offshore oil rig, and the Gulf was the center of American oil production in the 1970s and 1980s, when the worldwide price of crude soared into the stratosphere. The last governor to actually take on the industry was Huey Long in the 1930s.

In hindsight, you could argue that Louisiana became an oily banana republic, too dependent on drilling and refining, with too little emphasis on other more stable sources of jobs. At its peak in the 1970s, the oil and gas industry provided an astonishing 40 percent of state revenues. (Currently it's still a healthy 14 percent.) The century-long oil boom has also brought Third World–type problems to Louisiana, including the slow-motion environmental and structural degradation of the swamplands and coastal areas where much of the onshore drilling took place.

But the political system has also been long polluted by Big Oil and its big dollars—typified by the legendary populist Long, who won office by attacking the oil barons of Standard Oil but then steered lucrative oil leases to a company (with the memorable name of Win or Lose Oil) tied to himself and his cronies. In the mid-1980s, as Brackin and his co-workers in the DEQ were beginning their sweeping probe into NORM and radioactive pollution across Louisiana, the incumbent governor was the legendary silver-haired and acid-tongued archetype of all Louisiana politicians, Edwin Edwards.

A Democrat and a Cajun populist in the Huey Long tradition, Edwards had built his reputation on free-spending social programs paid for by sharply higher taxes on oil and gas revenues during the 1970's boom, but with the state suddenly struggling in the face of lower oil prices in the 1980s, the governor wasn't eager to curb production or penalize the industry. But the alleged corruption of the Edwards years—he was indicted but acquitted of felony charges in his ties to the nursing home industry—swept him out of office in 1987, replaced by the reform politics of Buddy Roemer.

Calling for "a Roemer revolution" and promising to "slay the dragon" of the Edwards administration, Louisiana's new governor shocked the system with an aggressive approach to environmental protection. He appointed a new boss to oversee Brackin and the other regulators at the DEQ—Dr. Paul Templet, a professor of environmental studies at my alma mater, LSU. Templet was a bona fide environmentalist who had organized the very first Earth Day on campus in Baton Rouge in 1970; shortly after that, he helped lead an effort to draft a Coastal Zone Enhancement Act for Louisiana, the first real effort to protect the state's wetlands after many years of abuse by Big Oil. Roemer turned to Templet as a key member of his transition team before taking office in January 1988, and it was during that time that Templet first began to learn that Louisiana had an extensive problem with TERM contamination, an issue he hadn't even heard of previously.

Like Brackin, Templet said he discovered that radioactive contamination in the Louisiana oil patch was so widespread that a radiation detector in a low-flying airplane was going off repeatedly as it passed over drilling fields and the pits where the industry had dumped a veritable sea of radium-laced wastewater. For Big Oil, it was a perfect storm—Brackin and his unit had been working on writing some of the toughest TERM-specific regulations in the country, and suddenly Louisiana had an environmental chief who was eager to enforce them and a governor who would stand behind him.

Brackin recalls today that Templet "was an environmentally conscious person who wanted to do the right thing without worrying about political consequences." He adds, after a pause: "Which is very unusual."

Upon taking office, Templet did something most unusual: He issued emergency rules declaring, in essence, that TERM was a public-health crisis in Louisiana. Oil and gas companies were now under orders to immediately inspect both their production equipment and their pipe-cleaning yards for radioactivity, and because it was an emergency rule, Templet and the DEQ were able to bypass the normal process of extensive public hearings and legislative oversight. Needless to say, Templet's maneuver—the only such emergency that was declared during the four years of the Roemer administration—was highly unpopular with the energy executives, and a foreshadowing of the bitter political battles that were to come.

But the hard-charging Louisiana regulators saw the emergency rules as merely the initial step to control the radioactive pollution across the state. At the time of the transition, Brackin was also working on new, permanent regulations for NORM that would treat the radium-laced waters and radioactive dust as a separate, highly controlled waste stream. That meant that wastes above a certain level of radioactive contamination would be required to undergo proper disposal, either at a site equipped to handle radioactive waste or through an approved and tightly regulated method such as deep well injection. It was a remarkable moment: Louisiana, which had spent much of the twentieth century as the lapdog for the oil and gas industry, was drawing up and promulgating the toughest standard for radioactive oil-field waste in the United States.

Indeed, despite the predictable opposition from industry lobbyists, Brackin, Templet, and the state DEQ won approval for the waste-stream regulations and implemented them by early 1992. By then, the effort that had been launched with Templet's emergency rule had identified some 29,000 sites across Louisiana with contamination from TERM. Not surprisingly, as Clark Street had learned in Mississippi, the DEQ agents also discovered cases where hot radioactive pipe had been donated for school playgrounds and other public venues. "One of my guys told me that if you sat on one of these pipes for an hour," Templet later recalled, "you could get your yearly dose of radiation." With support from the Roemer administration, Brackin's unit of state agents grew to roughly ten people, and in the early 1990s they fanned out across the state, writing up the worst offenders and ordering cleanups.

I first met Brackin shortly after the settlement in the Street case, at the time when I was taking on a number of new cases related to TERM. I was working out of my house and looking for office space, having left Jack Harang immediately after the Street trial. One of the worst cases of contamination I had seen was a pipe-cleaning yard outside of Lafayette, in the heart of Louisiana Cajun country, called 51 Oil Corp., which had been inspected under the new, tougher regulations after it was discovered that a worker had tracked radiation into his home. The DEQ had ordered 51 Oil to conduct an extensive and costly cleanup operation, and by the start of 1993 the owner of that small company, Jimmy Vanway, had hired me to sue his numerous oil and gas customers, to make them financially liable for the remediation as we had successfully done at the Street property in Laurel. So I met with Brackin to assure him, and the DEQ, that Vanway and 51 Oil were working to take care of the contamination. I was immediately impressed with his devotion to the cause of ridding Louisiana of TERM.

The suit we filed in the 51 Oil case was TERM's "shot heard 'round the world." We sued more than 100 oil companies that had sent pipe to 51 Oil, and demanded twenty million dollars in cleanup damages. Every major defense firm within fifty miles of New Orleans was quickly retained. We began taking the defendants' depositions and the other side was totally unprepared. I steamrolled them with all the knowledge I had gained on my previous cases. I will never forget the first big hearing we had when I walked into the courtroom with just myself and a paralegal and found it packed with more than 100 defense lawyers. Looking back, I probably should have felt intimidated by the scene, but I wasn't.

The presiding judge was Richard Ganucheau, who was a well-known no-nonsense jurist. My first big motion was to compel the oil companies to turn over all their radiation readings and tests throughout Louisiana, Mississippi, and Texas. They had denied that they had sent contaminated pipe to 51 Oil and so I had to go and prove it. The place to start would be their environmental records. They were aghast because if I got those records I would know where they had buried the waste all over those three states.

Then the notorious Ed Pickle, who had flown in from Houston for Shell Oil Company, appeared out of the blue. "Picklepatch" stood up and started arguing for all the oil companies that the information was not relevant and that this was a fishing expedition, etc., etc. Finally he got to the point and told the judge that if they gave me all this information, it would open them to a floodgate of litigation because I would start suing them all over the place. There was a grain of truth to that, but legally it amounted to a hill of beans. I will forever remember what came next. The judge said, "Mr. Pickle, do you know what I see in my courtroom?" Pickle responded no. The judge said, "What I see is a big fat elephant with a tick on its ass. Do you know who's the tick and who's the elephant? Produce the documents in ten days."

I never saw a madder rush of lawyers trying to get out to the hall so they could call their clients and give them the bad news. Needless to say they opened the checkbook after that, which meant that I had to get all those documents some other way in other cases.

Unfortunately, there were a lot of rich and powerful oil executives who didn't share my single-mindedness about cleaning up the oil patch. By the time I met Brackin, a massive pushback was well underway. Buddy Roemer was already out of the governor's mansion. In the 1991 election, Roemer's reform agenda had made powerful enemies, including the energy companies who didn't care for Templet's aggressive style of regulation at the DEQ. With Edwards— the darling of Cajuns, minorities, and other blue-collar voters—and white supremacist David Duke and his rabid base of rural right-wing supporters both on the ballot, Roemer didn't stand a chance. This was the election when Edwards famously said, "the only way I lose this election is if I'm caught in bed with either a live boy or a dead girl."

When Edwards returned to office in January 1992, he and his cronies began instantly turning the tide. Templet was replaced and Brackin's regulatory push was already doomed. There was no subtlety about it. In December of that year, Brackin's agents found radiation in three wells operated by a state legislator named Robert Adley out of Bossier City and wrote it up for an $1,800 fine. Adley and his allies in the legislature retaliated by dredging up a youthful indiscretion Brackin was involved in during his college days and introducing a bill that was aimed at getting him fired from the DEQ.

The bill to fire Brackin didn't pass, but that's probably because pro-business efforts in other arenas rendered it moot. The 51 Oil case particularly angered industry officials; they hated getting sued, and hated paying so quickly even more. There were children who lived right next door to the 51 Oil facility. At one point, Brackin had voiced his concern that kids were seen playing with a contaminated pipe, and he pointed out the known cancer risks of radium. Most folks would see that as responsible and concerned regulation, but it was too much for Big Oil. A top official of the Louisiana Independent Oil and Gas Association named Don Briggs publicly accused Brackin of practicing "eco-terrorism," adding: "Those kind of scare tactics and getting the community alarmed are not right."

At the same time, papers would later reveal that Exxon, along with the other oil majors, was aggressively lobbying the newly returned Edwards administration to ease up. At one meeting in which Brackin was present, an Exxon representative named John Rullman grew so furious with the regulator that he threw a chair against a wall and shattered it. Years later it emerged that during this time Rullman was having private meetings with Edwards.

The empire was striking back, and it was winning. Templet's replacement at the DEQ assured lawmaker Adley—the aggrieved well-owner—that Louisiana would indeed back off from its aggressive enforcement of the TERM regulations. When Templet returned to LSU, powerful energy executives who wield considerable clout at the state university first lobbied to get him fired and then succeeded in slashing his annual salary by $10,000, a petty move designed to remind Templet who was really in charge. When Brackin sought to enforce the new TERM regulations by inspecting a major oil-field waste operation on Bateman Island, he found himself on the losing end of a major turf war with another state agency, the Louisiana Department of Natural Resources, which has long been a pawn of the Big Oil interests.

A short time later, Brackin started to launch another investigation of a Big Oil icon, Texaco, after a report that the company had dumped barrels of TERM waste in Lake Salvador, a body of water southwest of New Orleans (the report was never proven or disproven). That was apparently too much for his new superiors at the DEQ. They called him in the next day and informed him he was going to get "cross-trained"—yes, that's really what they called it—by taking a leave from the TERM unit, as well as a temporary pay cut, and working for a time in the agency's hazardous-waste unit instead. He was gone for six months, and while he was away, he said, the DEQ returned more than $1 million in fines back to the oil companies; it also took the three state cars that his TERM agents used to cover the state from the DEQ headquarters in Baton Rouge and parceled them out to other units. By July 1994, according to a report in the *Times-Picayune*, almost all of the experienced TERM inspectors who'd worked closely with Brackin were fired, transferred, or left public service because they could see the writing on the wall.

"A career-ender" is what Brackin now calls taking on Big Oil. When his six months of "cross-training" in hazardous wastes were over, Brackin's bosses wanted him to go back to the now-neutered unit dealing with TERM, but he refused, much to their chagrin. He told them, "I don't want to go back because I will be seen as the guy who made it weaker," and he said he would have been beaten up by Louisiana's environmentalists for failing to carry out the rules that he himself had drafted. Brackin stayed with the DEQ for another sixteen years, retiring in 2010, but he never allowed himself to return to the job he loved best, taking on radioactive polluters.

Today, the stringent waste-stream regulations that Louisiana enacted in the early 1990s are still on the books and have even been updated, but unfortunately, they are also widely ignored, with little to no repercussions for not following them. Oil drillers in the state known officially as the Sportsmen's Paradise still pull up hot radium-226 from

deep underground, but Brackin says they typically mix and dilute the
wastes in large metal roll-off containers—not because that's safer for
the environment but because that allows them to dilute the radioactivity to levels below the DEQ regulation. More importantly, though,
there is little or no enforcement of the tough standard on the books—
rendering it almost completely impotent, just as the big-money oil and
gas interests had lobbied so intensely for.

"It's about greed," Brackin maintains, years after his departure
from enforcing the TERM regulations. He said the oil company lobbyists will fight any form of regulation, no matter how reasonable,
and then continue to fight the regulators if new laws or guidelines
somehow do make it onto the books. When the initial public outcry
and media frenzy over a problem like TERM dies down, as it inevita-
bly does, the self-interested parties are typically the ones left calling
the shots.

And the thing is, the cautionary tale of Richard Brackin was not
an isolated incident in the 1990s, during those chaotic early days
when regulators and a small group of environmental activists and
lawyers such as myself were on the trail of really doing something
about radioactive pollution. Across the oil-producing patch of the
Deep South, there were men and women like Brackin or Templet,
who'd come of age in the ecologically conscious era after the first
1970 Earth Day and who saw their job as preventing and cleaning up
pollution with honesty and integrity. But in one state after another,
these conscientious public servants were taken down, as the empire
of Big Oil fought back in a new era of free-market conservative economic policies.

"THE PEOPLE WHO MAKE THE DECISIONS"

In Kentucky, the state's top public radiation official was a regulator named John Volpe. In 1991, around the same time that concern over TERM was peaking in Louisiana, Volpe—who at the time was manager of Kentucky's radiation control program—got a call to inspect John Mullins's property in Martha, which had been contaminated by Ashland's careless, but at the time legal, disposal practices. Volpe broadened his investigation to look at other parcels in and around Martha that were showing elevated radiation levels, often because of "land farming," an environmentally careless practice in which Ashland was attempting to dilute radium-laced sludge or wastewater by mixing it with soil, which just polluted a wider area. Volpe's agency had not done a lot of work in the field of TERM before, but it seemed clear to this career regulator that the contamination spread across Martha was at a level high enough that it could impact the public's health.

But Volpe did not stay on the case long enough to mandate or oversee a cleanup of the mess that Ashland had created. Right after Volpe began looking more closely at contaminated properties in Martha, his politically appointed bosses at the state stepped in and took him off the case. "They didn't want a knowledgeable person involved in that," he later explained. The reason they cited was some outside consulting work that Volpe had done in neighboring Ohio, even though that project had nothing to do with TERM and had no bearing whatsoever on the work he was performing in Martha.

Volpe, like many environmental regulators, is brutally honest when he admits that the technical experts out in the field are not the ones calling the shots. "So the bottom line is—you've got to remember, these people, who are really hardworking individuals, don't make those decisions and so it really isn't the blame of the technical regulatory people that these types of things happen," he explained in an interview. "It really is this situation where you have the oil company here in Kentucky and the government entity on one side. I'm talking about the people who make the decisions." In the case of environmentally ravaged Martha, Kentucky, Volpe believes there is plenty of blame to go around, but the bottom line is that the politicians who receive tens of thousands of dollars in campaign contributions from Big Oil remain in control, and ultimately, they have to be the ones to enact and enforce any changes.

How did this affect my work as a trial lawyer taking on the goliaths of Big Oil inside a courtroom? Well, on one hand, the indifference of statehouse politicians to the environmental degradation of their states is one more reason why I exist. It's why the justice system is not just the arena of last resort but also sometimes the only resort a worker who's been poisoned his entire life or a rural landowner who suddenly finds that one of the world's most powerful corporations decided to use his backwoods as a radioactive trashcan has to fight on a nearly level playing field.

On the other hand, over the course of the 1990s as I tried more oil-patch cases in court, I found that the political indifference of the states could make life easier for Big Oil's high-paid lawyers; they would ask jurors, wouldn't their clients be facing severe regulatory penalties if they were doing something truly terrible? The successful political interference by the oil giants over the course of the 1990s was, to borrow a phrase from a popular legal thriller, a reversal of fortune, and a damn depressing one.

When Chevron capitulated in the Street case back in 1992, it was publicized in outlets such as the *New York Times* and the *MacNeil-Lehrer NewsHour*. I had assumed that such publicity would result in a push for more stringent regulation of TERM on the federal level by the EPA. After all, oil-field pollution was arguably a national problem, and hopefully Washington would rise above the petty politics of Southern statehouses, where something as minimal as an $1,800 fine could spark a quest for revenge. What's more, the administration of Democrat Bill Clinton, which took office in January 1993, had promised to reverse the sometimes embarrassingly pro-business environmental policies of Clinton's immediate predecessors, Ronald Reagan and George H.W. Bush.

But it turned out the die had already been cast at the end of the Reagan years. In 1982, after the initial discoveries of TERM in the North Sea oil field and elsewhere, Congress requested the EPA study the issue and then decide if these radioactive wastes from oil production should be regulated under the federal Superfund law that now controlled the disposal of toxic chemicals. This was, essentially, the idea that Richard Brackin would later try to advance in Louisiana, that there should be cradle-to-grave regulation of the oil-production waste stream; the notion that the public should be safeguarded from wastes that weren't only toxic but also laced with unsafe levels of radiation appeared to be a no-brainer. But the powerful energy lobby had already successfully kept oil-production waste out of the initial 1976 law known as the Resource Conservation and Recovery Act, or RCRA. Now, the EPA had waited until the last year of Reagan's presidency to rule on updating its regulations. It's important to remember that these years of federal delay and obfuscation in the mid-1980s were the same years that workers at the Street and the Case pipe-cleaning yards in Mississippi were systematically poisoned. In other words, incredibly, federal law at the time did not prohibit what we claimed Chevron had done in the Street and Case cases.

Maybe it didn't matter in the end because the results of the EPA review were profoundly, but predictably, disappointing. The EPA rationale for the exemption reads like it was pulled directly from oil-industry talking points or from the minutes of an American Petroleum Institute strategy meeting: " ... [RCRA] does not provide sufficient flexibility to consider costs and avoid the serious economic impacts that regulation would create for the industry's exploration and production operations..." Translation: America's thirst for (and addiction to) cheap oil is more important than protecting your health. To add insult to injury, the EPA claimed there was an adequate safeguard for the public: state and local governments. "Existing State and Federal regulatory programs are generally adequate for controlling oil, gas, and geothermal wastes," the agency reported, adding with remarkable bluntness, "Permitting delays would hinder new facilities, disrupting the search for new oil and gas deposits..." Risking lives was worth it so you wouldn't have to wait in a gas line. Shameful.

In 1989, the New Orleans *Times-Picayune* reported that the EPA's gutless move to tank on the TERM issue had saved Big Oil a whopping $6.7 billion. This reality should be a wake-up call to citizens who naively think that Washington will protect them from health hazards. The feds might act up when your kid's toy from China is laced with lead paint, but radiation dumping in small towns is OK when it's American oil barons on the hook for paying for the cleanup. The federal government has had numerous opportunities to regulate these dangerous oil-field wastes but instead has moved to exempt the energy industry from common-sense regulation again and again, from the Atomic Energy Act of 1954 and from RCRA and the Superfund laws. The few rules that do exist—Department of Transportation guidelines on shipping radioactive waste across state lines and some worker protections under the Occupational Safety and Health Administration—are not only flimsy but also rarely enforced. Even supposedly liberal administrations like those of Bill Clinton, or Barack Obama years later, have little interest in getting into a swordfight with Big Oil. The most insidious thing is that with its failure to regulate TERM, Washington and the EPA signaled that radioactive oil waste contamination is not important, which ensured a lack of coverage by our maddeningly fickle news media and a lack of awareness among the general public. It offered cover for state lawmakers, governors, and the bureaucrats to side with the energy lobby.

The last straw came in Mississippi, the same state where it all began. From the day that Chevron's expert H.T. Miller had showed up at Winston Street's pipe-rattling yard to size up the radioactive contamination there, oil-industry officials and their lobbyists have been scheming to avoid any regulations that would greatly increase their disposal costs or lead to costly cleanups at the sites they'd already polluted. In 1993, just months after the Street case was settled, the lobbyists pounced. With virtually no warning—just enough time for the state's radiological health official, Eddie Fuente, to deliver objections that were openly laughed at by lawmakers—the Mississippi Legislature stripped the regulation of TERM from the competent and aggressive regulators at the state Department of Health and handed it to a completely different body: the Oil and Gas Board.

This was the go-to ploy for Big Oil in every state where they could pull it off, and Mississippi was the crown jewel. You see, many states have a board or an agency that may sound like a public-interested regulatory body, but which in fact is designed to be on the side of industry. Thus, in Texas—historically the center of oil drilling in America, and thus where you would expect to find a significant TERM problem, officials quickly moved regulation of any radioactive oil-patch wastes to a panel called (wait for it) the Texas Railroad Commission. Decades ago, the state ceded regulation of pipelines—and thus the entire oil industry in the Lone Star State—to this powerful and industry friendly board. So any hope of dealing with TERM there was derailed...by the railroad commission.

In Mississippi, the Oil and Gas Board was similarly stacked with ex-industry officials and their allies, with nary an environmentalist in sight. Indeed, during the critical years for regulating TERM, the board's leader was Walter Boone, a retired Chevron employee! In case you have any doubts why the panel was created, its enabling legislation spells it out: "[T]o foster, encourage and promote the development, production and utilization of the natural resources of oil and gas in the state of Mississippi." Note the lack of language indicating any protection or disclosure for the general public. That just wasn't important.

After the 1993 legislation was enacted, the Mississippi Oil and Gas Board did nothing for six long years. And when the panel did finally take action, it was to protect the oil industry that had poisoned Mississippians like the pregnant Karen Street and the workers at Winston Street's pipe yard. First up was its Rule 69 to regulate ongoing operations in the oil patch, a measure so weak that our expert Marvin Resnikoff testified that it actually allowed workers to be exposed to more radiation than permitted by the existing EPA or federal Nuclear Regulatory Commission guidelines. Once that passed, the board went back to Rule 68, its proposal dealing with the cleanup and disposal of radioactive wastes that had been improperly buried in the past. Here, incredibly, the solution of the Mississippi Oil and Gas Board was, quite simply, to ratify the shoddy practices of yesteryear, based on what the industry called "land farming," that heinous practice of mixing radium-laced soil into clean dirt. In other words, the pollution isn't removed but instead is spread across a much wider area! The Oil and Gas Board's solution to pollution was dilution. Spreading the risk around and dispersing the waste through the food chain, just as H.T. Miller had suggested in one of his papers on TERM.

My team of experts and environmentalists weren't the only ones appalled by Rule 68. In fact, in 1999 the EPA actually stepped in and explicitly warned Mississippi that the "land spreading" practice was a violation of federal hazardous-waste laws—in essence, creating new Superfund sites across the Magnolia State. "We believe that Revised Rule 68 would not protect public health," EPA Regional Administrator John Hankinson Jr. wrote the board. "Rather, it would allow the spread of radioactive contamination throughout many areas in the state of Mississippi." The Oil and Gas Board tossed out the EPA letter because EPA would not come and testify at its just-for-show kangaroo proceedings that had no regard for actual fairness or justice.

The Revised Rule 68 was approved a short time later. We appealed its implementation and we also tried to get the U.S. Attorney for Mississippi to sue to block it from ever taking effect, in light of the EPA letters to the Oil and Gas Board suggesting that the state measures contradicted federal law. But he refused—more proof that his boss President Clinton was not the ardent environmentalist he claimed to be. I later came to know that the oil fields of southern Arkansas are some of the most polluted in the country. When I asked a local if Clinton tried to do anything when he was governor to clean it up, he laughed at me. Believe it or not after a decade of appeals the Mississippi Supreme Court threw out Rule 68 and ordered the Oil and Gas Board back to the drawing board. The oil industry has asked for rehearing, which is pending as of the writing of this book.

But incredibly, things got even worse in Mississippi. And the trigger was Brookhaven, the epicenter of radioactive contamination in the state. There, we had sued Chevron on behalf of another landowner named Alcus Smith. It was a textbook open-and-shut case—the evidence was undisputed that the giant oil company had dumped radioactive oil-field waste on the Smith property, and after a three-week trial the jury ordered Chevron to pay $2.3 million to clean it up. But Chevron appealed the verdict all the way to the Mississippi Supreme Court, where a truly remarkable thing happened: The high court tossed out the judgment because Smith had failed to exhaust all his administrative remedies for relief before the industry-favoring Mississippi Oil and Gas Board. The courthouse doors closed to injured landowners in Mississippi—and remain so today.

The ruling was unprecedented. It stunned the legal community, and it had a very real effect on Mississippi families that had been dumped on by Big Oil and that were desperately seeking justice. One of the citizens left in the cold was a lifelong Mississippian named Gerald Donald. Donald had bought a twenty-acre property in Wayne County at a foreclosure sale and let the previous owners, the Davis brothers, continue to operate their business there. What Donald didn't know was that the Davis's business, allegedly, was draining the sludge from massive wastewater pits in the oil patch and dumping the wastes on the property. In 1995, Donald discovered his property was contaminated with radium, and he sued the brothers, only to have the case thrown out of court after the state Supreme Court ruling. In fact, Donald passed away in 2005 without getting justice. That didn't end the matter; his daughter, Stephanie Howard, has been carrying on, pleading in vain for years with the Oil and Gas Board to take up the matter as a first step toward justice.

I press on with these cases, reminded of the words of Dr. Martin Luther King Jr., who said that "the arc of the moral universe is long but it bends toward justice." In Mississippi, for the residents of a string of small rural towns that were poisoned by the carelessness of Big Oil, that moral arc remains badly broken.

The start of a new century was a low point—for the cause of cleaning up decades of pollution left behind by the oil companies, to be sure, but also for me as a trial lawyer. Nearly a decade had passed since the intoxicating finale of the Street trial, which I had viewed not only as vindication for my clients but as opening wide a door of environmental law, seeking justice for everyday folks who didn't have a friend in the stacked political system. I guess that on some level, I fully expected the oil giants and their silk-suited attorneys to fight like hell to slam that door back in my face. But what I hadn't counted on was the level to which elected officials and their hand-picked appointees would collude with the corporations and against the people.

Make no mistake, I was doing fine financially. In 1997, Barry and I moved into a grand old home with a central courtyard and

Stuart and Barry at their home in the French Quarter.

a glorious central staircase in the heart of the French Quarter, just a stone's throw from the Mississippi River levees and the aroma of hot beignets and chicory coffee at Café du Monde. I had a new law partner, Andrew Sacks, whom I'd teamed up with a couple of years after parting ways with Jack Harang. I was doing TERM cases almost exclusively, and I won or gained favorable settlements in enough of them to create my own niche in the legal community. But I wanted more, and the situation in Mississippi, the state where I'd had my big breakthrough, was particularly frustrating to me, almost painful.

The bottom line is that after our initial success against Chevron, Big Oil had run me out of the state of Mississippi. By the year 2000, the slights were piling up: the silencing of Richard Brackin and any serious environmental enforcement in states such as Louisiana and Kentucky, the stonewall approach in states like Texas, the mindboggling indifference of the federal government, and now the blatant endorsement of corporate pollution in Mississippi. But the good thing I've learned about the law in this country is that when one door closes, another one usually opens. In Louisiana, the powerful legal community has often served as a counterbalance to government-sanctioned injustice. Unlike Mississippi, the courts in my home state had not completely blocked our ability to sue the polluters. And at the turn of the millennium, a new case presented itself that at first seemed fairly routine, but was actually stunningly audacious.

In a New Orleans courtroom, we were about to take on the world's most powerful corporation. And this time, we were going to take it all the way to the jury.

This one was for all the marbles.

BIG OIL
AND THE SINGLE DIGIT

A GOOD TIME TO BEGIN telling the story of the humble, mostly black, working-poor, but proud Mississippi River town of Harvey, Louisiana—and the shocking arrogance of the world's largest oil company—is on a day back around 1987.

Workers for a firm called Intracoastal Tubular Corp., or ITCO—sweaty men, some of them caked in white silty dust—straggled in from the busy pipe-strewn yard to watch a training video. It had been produced and sent to them by ITCO's biggest-by-far customer: the oil giant Exxon Corporation, which had sent out tens of thousands of pipes to get cleaned at this yard near the big canal in Harvey over a number of years. The purpose of the video, according to the script, was "Exxon Company U.S.A. Production Department Training."

The film was called *Naturally Occurring Low-Level Radiation in Oil and Gas Production*. Actually, it was originally just called *Naturally Occurring Radiation in Oil and Gas Production*—someone at Exxon had penciled in the additional words "low-level" in a scrawl across the top of the script. That was one of the many things that we uncovered many years later, while suing Exxon. Someone obviously thought that they could whitewash the oil company's liability problem with radioactive waste by throwing in as many soothing, reassuring words as possible. The real purpose, after all, was not to improve safety but to assuage workers who might otherwise be shocked to learn after ten, twenty, thirty years of cleaning hot pipe around a dusty yard that the dust was actually a silent, deadly poison, and who might want to sue them.

But getting back to the 1980s, an ITCO employee slips the tape into the VCR and the feature presentation begins. "Montage of city, people, trees, whatever," the original script reads—anything, I guess, to distract the audience. Then a narrator appears on the screen, walking down a trail through thick, lovely woodlands with birds chirping and the occasional butterfly fluttering across the screen, and a pristine oil rig just barely visible through the dense tree line. You half expected a colorful bird to land on the narrator's shoulder. Instead, the man speaks:

> We may not think about it much, but radiation is an everyday fact of life. Now we're not talking about the "Chernobyl" kind of radiation that makes headlines. This radiation is a much lower level, everyday garden variety that occurs naturally, all around us. In fact you'll find it in the garden. And in the sunshine, and the trees, and in the very ground we build our houses on, and it's in us. From the day we're born.

The opening statement was larded with errors of omission and commission, and it went downhill from there. *Naturally Occurring*

Low-Level Radiation in Oil and Gas Production failed to mention that the naturally occurring radiation that the workers at the ITCO facility dealt with—highly concentrated scale, thick with radium-226—is one of the more lethal substances that an American worker has ever been exposed to on a daily basis. Besides, chirping birds can't drown out the fact that any kind of radiation—even that bright and cheery radiation from the sun—can be harmful.

But, again, that would be pretending that the real purpose of this training video was to actually train, to inform, to keep workers safe and protected. But you don't have to be a petro-chemical scientist to see that the real purpose of *Naturally Occurring Low-Level Radiation in Oil and Gas Production* was to attempt to limit corporate liability while reassuring any workers who might have begun hearing rumblings on the news about radioactivity and oil in the late 1980s. It was born from the very same instinct to brand this poisonous and concentrated radium that was getting yanked out of the earth as NORM, as something perfectly "normal" rather than a dangerous by-product of humankind's addiction to fossil fuels. But to get to that place, Exxon and its hired operatives had to tell some real whoppers to workers like the crew in Harvey, Louisiana. Again, the narrator:

> *We've known about the presence of naturally occurring low-level radiation in some gas plants since the early 1970s. Since then, safety procedures have been developed for the limited number of facilities that are affected. Last year several companies, including Exxon, began to more closely monitor their oil and gas processing facilities. We have found small amounts of radiation in some of our field operations, and we have decided to expand the testing program. In the coming months, you may see someone at work taking measurements.*

Around our law office, we called it the "chirping birds and butterflies video"—a movie classic in Big Oil's crusade to downplay its

TERM pollution. Meanwhile, things would not turn out so rosy for some of the workers in Harvey who saw the film or worked there in the 1980s. Some of them were on the verge of getting very, very sick, like a man I met in the late 1990s called Milton Vercher. By then, he was already in the middle of a long battle with leukemia, and he had many former co-workers battling illnesses of similar severity.

Vercher had come down to New Orleans as young high school grad from northern Louisiana in the late 1950s when the waterways of the Crescent City were booming, and for two decades he made a decent living at ITCO cleaning out miles of pipe. But by 1996, with cancer cells taking over his body, Vercher was too weak to continue working.

Milton Vercher's cancer set the stage for what would be the climactic legal battle in our long fight against Big Oil and its radioactive trail of pollution, and it would play out right here in New Orleans, where my story began. As the calendar flipped from the twentieth century to the twenty-first, the chain of events that was triggered in that dusty pipe yard on the Westbank of the Mississippi set us on a courtroom collision course with the biggest oil company of them all, where a jury of twelve Americans would get to finally pass judgment on Exxon's long record of dumping on a modest, working-class Louisiana town. None of this would have happened were it not for the astounding arrogance of the corporation, now writ larger as the merged ExxonMobil, and its lawyers.

There was a time, early on, when we would have recommended accepting as little as $10 million on behalf of our client, Judge Joseph Grefer—the man who owned the twenty-two acres of land in Harvey where ITCO had operated. When Exxon canceled three mediations and then refused to consider what seemed like a modest sum (especially in light of the massive radioactive pollution Grefer's property had suffered), our legal team and our clients decided that we would make them pay, and that we would go for all of the marbles, as it were.

We would ask the jury for an award of $3 billion dollars, with the hope that $1 billion wasn't out of the question.

If we lost to ExxonMobil and its top-dollar attorneys, we might not get one thin dime.

All or nothing. Somewhere, my gambling man of a father had to be looking down at this bet and smiling.

TAKING ON "THE DEATH STAR"

The story of Exxon begins nearly a century and a half ago; the hubris and arrogance that flow through the company's bloodlines are as thick as the billions of barrels of oil that it has pumped into the world's economy. It begins with the greatest robber baron of the nineteenth-century Gilded Age, John D. Rockefeller. A Cleveland bookkeeper who realized the amazing income-producing potential of oil roughly a decade after the first gusher in rural upstate Pennsylvania, the dour-faced Rockefeller founded Standard Oil in 1870 and within a few short years, he dominated the industry with a ruthlessness that belied his modest, church-going persona.

Rockefeller's real talent was in creating a vast monopoly; he conspired with railroads and other shippers to win low prices for Standard Oil and to force rivals out of the market for petroleum products. The exploitation of the original Pennsylvania oil fields established the pattern of boom and pollution-laden bust that lasts to this day, as nineteenth-century writers spoke of foul-smelling oil creeks, how "mud, deep, and indescribably disgusting, covered all the main and by-roads in wet weather..." in devastated rural pockets of the Keystone State.

During the twentieth century, a dizzying series of antitrust law-suits and corporate mergers obscured the fact that Exxon, created by one of the bigger mergers in 1973, was the corporate heir to the dubious legacy of Rockefeller's Standard Oil. Along the Gulf, a com-pany called Humble Oil, which was created in East Texas in 1911 in the afterglow of the famous Texas "gusher," Spindletop, had allied itself with the Rockefellers and a key Standard Oil affiliate, becom-ing the grandfather to Exxon. Humble was the company that placed the first offshore rig off Louisiana in 1948, a pioneer in exploration that pulled up millions of barrels of oil in the Deep South, along with tons of radium-226.

It's hard to find the right adjectives or turn of phrase to describe the sheer power of this global corporation, especially after it merged with one of its leading rivals to form the behemoth ExxonMobil in 1999. In 2012, with prices at the gas pump surging and American motorists addicted to their cars, ExxonMobil raked in nearly a bil-lion dollars in pure profit a week, amounting to $41 billion for the entire year. In that same year, the Pulitzer Prize–winning journalist and author Steve Coll called ExxonMobil "a corporate state within the American state" and "one of the most powerful businesses ever produced by American capitalism." It wasn't just a matter of cash but also culture—intensely secretive, not afraid to butt into messy wars and conflicts overseas or to harass scientists who advance a theory of global warming that posed a threat to ExxonMobil's longtime strat-egy of expanding the worldwide use of fossil fuel in perpetuity. Even some company insiders jokingly call the firm's opulent, futuristic headquarters near Dallas "the Death Star" or "the God Pod."

But as anyone who's ever cracked open a Greek tragedy probably knows, the sin of hubris can be a lethal flaw, that tiny vent hole in the Death Star.

ExxonMobil certainly treated the blue-collar workers at the ITCO facility with arrogance that soon evolved into cruelty. The Grefer family had first leased their land in Harvey to ITCO and its owner John Hooper, a family friend, in the 1950s when the Gulf oil boom was really taking off. At its peak, ITCO was a $30 million company that operated a fleet of 120 trucks in the Louisiana oil patch, and it handled an estimated 20,000 to 30,000 tons of pipe. Although Exxon wasn't the only ITCO customer, it was by far the largest, so much so that Exxon even had an office and some full-time employees at the site. Apparently none of them had the job of telling ITCO's blue-collar workers out in the yard that the pipe they were cleaning was highly radioactive.

After the whole ITCO enterprise had collapsed, right around the time of the industry-wide TERM disclosures of the mid-to-late 1980s, our firm took on Milton Vercher's case. After leaving ITCO Milton had gone to work at another pipe yard called Alpha Technical. In investigating the case, we required Alpha to produce its property for inspection. However, like that Shell property in Mississippi it was clean as a whistle. DEQ records showed no permits for a cleanup at the site. Our consultant decided to jump the fence to check out the adjoining property over the hysterical objection of Alpha's owner. Sure enough the meters went off within feet of the fence. Radioactive material was in their neighbor's yard and we believed Alpha had bulldozed it. Unfortunately for them and Exxon, the property was owned by a retired judge, Joseph Grefer. We asked the Grefer family, who had owned the land for a century, for permission to extensively test their property in Harvey where Milton Vercher had worked. As we expected, the long plot that ran many blocks through the heart of Harvey, now abandoned and thick with green overgrown grass, was highly contaminated with radium. Judge Grefer had a well-deserved reputation as a no-nonsense jurist and he was very angry when he found out that the family property was radioactive. So we worked with Judge Grefer to bring a case against Exxon—not only to make them pay for the considerable cost of restoring the property, but also to seek punitive damages for such careless behavior by such a wealthy corporation.

And the more that we talked to some of Vercher's colleagues from the pipe yard, the more we learned how outrageous Exxon's conduct really was.

Melvin Thomassie Jr. was hired by ITCO in 1980 and worked at the company for ten years, as a rigger hooking and rolling pipes, as a crane operator, and as a truck driver. Years later, he recalled in an interview what happened at the yard when they rattled the pipe, the same process that had caused so many problems at the Street facility in Laurel. "It hits the ground or goes straight up in the air and the wind blew it around. The whole ground was always covered, for many years. Even the racks, everything was covered, the crane, your suit, your truck, your clothing." Yet despite this, Thomassie said there was no special washing facility at ITCO. The workers simply went home caked in stuff that they had no idea was so hazardous to their health.

In fact, when Thomassie worked there in the 1980s, the Exxon PR offensive had done such a good job that the owners and top bosses at the yard, including ITCO founder and boss, John Hooper, actually bought into Exxon's baloney that all the scale and the dust swirling around was completely harmless. "They took us all to lunch one day," said Thomassie, recalling what happened in 1987. "You know, bullshitted us that you get more harm out of watching television than you would breathing this dust. And, you know, pretty much, a lot of the old-timers, they will believe it." As a result, he recalled, some workers actually stopped wearing masks and other protective gear—the exact opposite of the message they should have received. Why wear a mask when it was like watching TV, or sunbathing?

At the time of the video, his father, Melvin Thomassie Sr.—who'd worked at ITCO for thirty-two years, including fifteen as a foreman cutting open pipe—was in good health. A few years later, Thomassie's dad became ill and died of pancreatic cancer in 1999.

Horace Fennidy, who worked at the ITCO site from 1980 to 1986, at the height of the oil boom, recalled the grimy working conditions there. "It was white dust," he said of the radioactive scale. "It was like fine particles, like crystal, little crystals flying out of the pipe everywhere. I mean it was something, because to go to work you had to have two pair of clothes. I had coveralls that I'd wear over my regular clothes because I couldn't go home all covered in that stuff. You were too dusty by the end of the day."

As we got deeper into researching the Grefer claim, we also learned that while the blue-collar workers were getting confused but calming messages about the dust they were bringing home every night, there was increasing panic up in the corporate suites. It turned out that while the employees were rattling pipe without masks or gloves, the world's biggest oil company was eager to cut its ties with ITCO, divesting itself of a huge liability.

On March 27, 1987, John Hooper got a phone call summoning him to a meeting at Exxon's posh high-rise office in downtown New Orleans to discuss "an issue" that had arisen at the ITCO facility. When Hooper got there, he was ushered into a room with men in suits whom he'd never seen in all his years cleaning pipes. They introduced themselves as Lindsay Booher, an industrial hygienist for Exxon, and John Rullman, who identified himself as a director of governmental and regulatory affairs; in other words, a lobbyist. They were not the guys who get called in to make workers healthier. These were the guys who try to put out political fires. Rullman, you'll recall, was the guy who smashed a chair on the wall at the DEQ when meeting with Richard Brackin and who had private meetings with Governor Edwin Edwards.

The secret backstory to this March 1987 meeting is eleven months of sheer corporate panic, eleven long months when blue-collar workers like Melvin Thomassie Jr. breathed, ingested, and wore home poison dust while rich men in penthouse offices scurried like cockroaches to get their story straight.

Remember, the industry cover-up of the TERM crisis happened on two levels. There were the decades when a small circle of oil-patch engineers, their bosses, and industry "health experts" like H.T. Miller knew there was a huge radioactivity problem but managed to keep things buried deep in the back of Big Oil's cluttered file cabinets. But everything changed in the spring of 1986, when Chevron was forced to come clean about the radiation in the Raleigh field and the contamination of the Street and Case pipe-yard properties. The news about the Streets, their lawsuit against Shell and Chevron seeking $35 million, and the growing involvement of state regulators like Eddie Fuente in Mississippi and Richard Brackin in Louisiana sent shockwaves through Big Oil's back offices.

In the spring of 1986, Howard Collier, the manager of regulatory affairs for Exxon, wrote a memo to his higher-ups about the enormous risk to the company from the situation that was playing out in Laurel. The big picture for Exxon and for the entire industry was the risk of increased regulation. "Chevron's discovery is nothing new... my primary concern is that the current investigation and analysis not unduly influence the EPA, who is in the process of deciding, under RCRA [the Resource Conservation and Recovery Act of 1976, an environmental statute which regulates the disposal of hazardous waste] whether Exxon's radioactive produced water should be classified as a hazardous waste and handled as such." The increased measures to properly dispose of TERM would have cost the industry more than $1 billion in just the first four years, industry officials estimated, and so EPA regulation was to be avoided at all costs.

But Exxon also had a more immediate concern—the liability for the ongoing work at its own primary pipe-cleaning yard in the region, which was the ITCO site in Harvey. In the fall of 1986, the lobbyist Rullman sent a "confidential report" to his superiors in which he warned them, citing the situation up in Mississippi, that "ITCO is a potential 'look-alike' to Street," and that Exxon should "perform low-key radiation exposure measurements" in Harvey and try to carry out mitigation procedures before those measurements were taken." In plain English, Rullman wanted Exxon to clean up the site from its highly radioactive state of the mid-1980s, and then conduct the field tests, making sure everything was "low key" so as not to set off any alarms.

And that wasn't all. In the same "confidential memo," Rullman advises that "continued use of the ITCO yard could complicate any potential personal injury liability claims since it would be difficult to determine when the exposure occurred that caused the injury." What the lobbyist was really saying, in cold legalese, was that Exxon needed to stop doing business with ITCO, even though that might mean shutting the small company down and putting all its employees on the unemployment line. Basically, Rullman wanted the world's most profitable, $1-billion-a-week company to increase its distance from a handful of salt-of-the-earth workers who were barely making a middle-class wage laboring in a cloud of poisonous dust, simply to make sure it avoided any responsibility for the doctors' bills when (because they knew it was only a matter of time) these workers started getting bone disease or cancer.

The urgent meeting that Hooper was summoned to in New Orleans was all part of the grand plan, a scene from a carefully scripted and staged play. In the months that followed, the ITCO founder returned to Harvey and spent several thousand dollars to install what at that time was a state-of-the-art, enclosed cleaning system that finally included a vacuum to suck up all the stray dust. But there were delays in getting final approval to turn the device on, and soon it wouldn't matter much. Exxon had slowed the flow of pipe into the ITCO yard down to a trickle—exactly the strategy that Rullman had urged in his top secret memo. By the start of the 1990s, ITCO was bankrupt.

Exxon's conduct was appalling, and heartless. Its plan was to scatter the former ITCO workers at different jobs, so that if they became ill at some later date—and radiation-related illnesses often take years to develop—it would be more difficult to trace the cause, and the legal liability, back to Exxon's hot pipes. What's more, the workers would not be together at the lunch table sharing their stories or connecting the dots back to Exxon or the white dust. Adding insult to injury, the end of ITCO would mean that these blue-collar workers who'd been contaminated day after day now had to look for a job at the height of the George H.W. Bush–era recession. There was no talk in any of Exxon's private papers of seeking medical treatment for, or assessing the health of, the people who worked for ITCO, or really any hint of humanity whatsoever.

But Exxon's venal strategy was also flawed. There was no way for the company to keep the lid on its contamination of the ITCO site, especially after workers like Milton Vercher fell seriously ill. I was now working with a new law partner, Michael Stag, who had been a friend and classmate of my partner Barry in the MBA program at Loyola in the mid-1990s. When we decided to take on the cases of the worker Vercher and then the property owner Grefer, the Exxon matter seemed a sad but routine matter—headed for a settlement just like the Street case, or the Case matter in Brookhaven or the Martha, Kentucky, case.

It turned out to be anything but routine.

"THIS IS OUR SHOT"

We were shocked when ExxonMobil refused to bargain with us. Like Chevron at the start of the Street case, they must have thought they

Stuart with new law partner Michael Stag.

could "out-lawyer" us. My partner Mike Stag's theory was that this area of environmental law was still new enough that the oil giant's attorneys simply didn't know what they were getting into. "They had this strange theory," he recalled, "that because people had dumped old tires on some of the property, that it wasn't worth cleaning up."

They had assigned two lawyers to the case; one was a female attorney who had been an in-house council for a number of years and had recently left to join a private firm. It was clear when we reached out to them during the pre-trial discovery period that the lawyers in New Orleans were not the ones calling the shots. Instead, their corporate bosses back in Texas could not have cared less that their Big Oil sisters like Chevron had finally settled up when confronted with the evidence of their wrongdoing. Instead, they had already made known their contempt for what they considered a dirty, blue-collar backwater burg in Harvey. Newly merged to form ExxonMobil at the turn of the millennium, they were the 800-pound gorilla of corporate America, and they did not settle.

The trial was initially set for December 2000, at the end of that crazy autumn when the nation was riveted by the hanging chads and the Florida recount of the Bush-Gore presidential election. As our jury trial was just about to commence, ExxonMobil's lawyer Patricia Weeks came up to us and asked, "What's your bottom line?" By now, we had assembled a team of attorneys to do battle with ExxonMobil and had invested considerable time and dollars in poring through the discovery documents, in taking depositions from the key witnesses, and on conducting extensive environmental testing. Although we would have settled for even less at the very outset, after a huddle in an adjacent courtroom with the team and the judge we asked for $13 million.

We still would likely have settled for $10 million.

Weeks said she would have to call her clients and run this by them. All of this was occurring while the prospective jurors were lined up in the hall awaiting jury selection. I could see her passing down the hall clearly agitated as she spoke on her cellular phone. When she returned, obviously distraught, she told me she wanted to see the judge in chambers. I refused to have a private conversation with the court, so my co-counsel Ron Austin accompanied me into the chambers. The oil company apparently wanted to take the case to trial, but then Weeks blurted out that she wasn't prepared to do that. She asked Judge Gill-Jefferson for a continuance, which the judge indicated she would not do.

In front of us and the judge, this high-powered attorney suddenly burst into uncontrollable tears and began making loud moaning sounds, announcing that she had emotional issues that her client was unaware of. She was not ready to begin the trial. She began to sob. Her crying was so loud that law clerks and secretaries rushed down to see what was going on. In my then-fifteen years of practicing law, I had never seen nor heard of anything like it. Just minutes earlier, she had seemed stone-cold rational. But now ExxonMobil's lead counsel—finally realizing she would have to defend the oil company's conduct before a jury of twelve everyday citizens of Greater New Orleans—was having what appeared to be a complete nervous breakdown. Her partners were called in to see what was going on. They rushed down the hallway and realized that they may be trying this case totally unprepared. I was familiar with these guys, hard-nosed experienced defense litigators from the firm that I had joined right after law school. I would love to have been a fly on the wall when they got her back to their conference rooms. In fact, Weeks was forced to leave within weeks and formed her own firm.

Unfortunately, there was little that Judge Gill-Jefferson could do. The trial was pushed back until April of 2001. I was devastated. We had worked twelve hours a day, seven days a week, getting ready for this trial. The lost time and money was enormous since we would have to prepare for trial all over again.

Now, of course, our $13 million offer was off the table. As the new trial date drew closer, we got a call from one of ExxonMobil's other lawyers, curious to know if our proposed deal was still on the table. We told him no and that now, we would not settle for anything less than $26 million.

But the reality was that I was beginning to relish taking the case all the way to the jury, and so were my co-counsel in the case. It was Jack Harang who once told me: "Settlements are like kissing your sister; it feels good but isn't very sexy." He was right, of course—it had been more than eight years now since we'd settled the Street case with Chevron, and after all the ups and downs I was ready for a legal Battle of New Orleans, a win-or-lose showdown.

As we were walking toward the Orleans Parish courthouse, past the tall steel skyscrapers of Poydras Street, I turned to my law partner Mike Stag, bursting with adrenalin.

"This is our shot," I said to him. "You will never have the world's largest, richest company defenseless in civil court in New Orleans again." I was surer than ever that ExxonMobil's lawyers were completely incompetent and the only issue now was how much to settle for. The reason: ExxonMobil's lawyers were babes in the woods compared to us after what we had learned about TERM and the laws surrounding it in the six months of the Street trial.

Indeed, as our collision course with ExxonMobil grew inevitable, we had worked to assemble something of our own dream team of New Orleans trial lawyers to do battle with the oil giant. In fact, I had made peace with Jack, and asked if he would join the team. Despite our past personal differences, I had learned during the Street trial that we could be quite a one-two punch inside a courtroom—with my persistence in getting the most from our own scientific experts and doing battle with the experts on the other side, and with Jack's folksy, likable manner with a jury and regular folks in the witness box. I still have yet to meet the trial lawyer who can top Jack in making a killer opening and closing argument—and for this case we were going to need every weapon in our arsenal.

Our final group included six lawyers, including a valuable contribution from my partner Barry Cooper, who was there to share my biggest challenge in a courtroom. Another key player was Ron Austin, a young up-and-coming attorney whom I'd worked with on the Gaylord Tank Fire Case during the 1990s. Ron was a local product like me, having grown up in Jefferson Parish on the Westbank of the Mississippi, a stone's throw from the ITCO site. I used to tell him, "If you want to swim with the sharks, you're going to get bit." In the Grefer case, Ron's key tasks would include heading up the jury selection, helping us find twelve men and women who would give our argument the best shake, as well as helping Jack with the arguments.

As we discussed strategy, we agreed there's a big difference between seeking a settlement with a massive global corporation and taking them to trial. As Ron recalled, "We probably could have settled the case for $10 million—had ExxonMobil's legal counsel not been so arrogant." Now we had those bigger, billion-dollar numbers in mind.

Audacious? Perhaps. In 2001, there had only been five times in the entire then-225-year history of the United States in which a jury had awarded more than $1 billion, and none of those had been for this particular kind of case, for damaging an individual property as we were alleging in the Grefer suit. But outrageous? No. Consider the target. The purpose of punitive damages is, quite simply, to punish, to make a big corporation like ExxonMobil think twice before it casually poisons its workers. For the world's biggest oil company, one that now makes $1 billion every eight days or so, even $100 million would just be a bug on the windshield of justice.

Indeed, Austin still recalls that during the process of *voir dire* (jury selection), his primary goal was twofold: to accustom would-be jurors to the notion that $1 billion was a reasonable finding against ExxonMobil, and then to get those folks on the final panel. We knew that ExxonMobil's lawyers would employ the same "dose dancing" technique that Chevron's attorney had used, and we wanted jurors who might be immune to their numbers racket.

"I wanted to relate to the jury pool what the radiation meant to them in their everyday lives," Ron recalled later. "You know, there was someone on the jury who enjoyed her garden, so it would be important to her, the fact that there was radiation in the ground." He said the same was true for prospective jurors whose own kids might play in the backyard, just as children played near the ITCO parcel in

Harvey. "That was my game plan," he said, "getting a jury who could deal with it and not get caught up in the science."

When the trial finally opened on April 17, 2001, we tried to keep things on that basic level and remind the jury constantly that this was a simple matter of justice. In taking the case against ExxonMobil all the way, I'm sure it was in the back of my mind that if we won, this could be the crowning achievement of my career, or that it would vindicate our focus on radioactive oil pollution. But that's not really how the brain of the tort lawyer is wired—not when it's the first quarter of the big game and you're slugging it out in the trenches and the adrenalin is coursing through your veins. No, it was hunt for the big "kill" that really had me jacked up.

Jack told the jurors that this would be a case of "us"—the regular folks who live in a community like Harvey, Louisiana—versus "them," the all-powerful, profit-sucking Big Oil icon. There was "a deep, dark, evil thing going on, ladies and gentlemen, that was happening to the Grefers, the people that owned ITCO," Jack told the jury that morning. "And those folks knew nothing about it, but Exxon and their predecessor companies did. The pipe that they were pulling out of oil wells quite often contained highly radioactive material."

By the time that Jack got to the part where he told the jurors about the "chirping birds and butterflies" video, he was really rolling. He strove to paint the executives at ExxonMobil as not just careless but as snooty out-of-towners who had committed the greatest possible sin in the eyes of these Southern men and women—they had looked down on them.

"You know, ladies and gentlemen, by their actions, by their reckless handling of this toxic waste, they have shown to us that they believed that their actions, that they were bigger than this court . . . bigger than this state, and certainly bigger than the poor people of this property and the business that they destroyed. It's going to be up to you, ladies and gentlemen, to teach them that the cost of doing good is less than the cost of doing bad, that it's cheaper to do right than it is to do wrong. And make them pay a full measure for what they've done. What Exxon's done is committed an environmental rape on the property of the Grefers and the property that was operated by ITCO."

In response to Jack's moving statement about injustice, about ExxonMobil's pride and prejudice, if you will, ExxonMobil's lawyers tried to make the Grefer case all about the numbers (their slanted numbers, of course) and about the dollars. Remarkably, the representatives of the world's most profitable company claimed that the Grefers were the greedy party in Harvey and might take the money and buy an island in Tahiti. They claimed the real cost of cleaning up the Grefer property was only $46,000, even after we'd established through expert testimony that the contamination was far worse, and they had spent more than $200,000 just testing it. And jurors had to wonder that if cleaning up the radium at the site was such a simple, low-cost matter, then why did ExxonMobil not do it, rather than let workers take their daily lunch break on benches covered in toxic dust?

The trial took five-and-a-half weeks. My job, for the most part, was to flesh out Jack's pretty words with the facts and the hard science. I would be handling all of the ExxonMobil witnesses on cross-examination and all of the expert testimony. I carried out the direct examination of our witnesses, including Richard Brackin, the long-muzzled Louisiana state official. He told the jury about Rullman's chair-breaking incident and that ExxonMobil had broken the law. I also examined Stan Waligora, whose credentials on radiological health were unimpeachable. I did my best to pick apart their experts on cross-examination. It had been a dozen years since I'd signed onto the Street case in Mississippi knowing next to nothing about radioactivity. Now, I had a thick pyramid of knowledge, about not only the alarming health impacts of exposure to radium but also Big Oil's decades of awareness. In this case against ExxonMobil, we could add the warning from the early 1950s from the firm's medical director, which was ignored by his bosses. It was grueling work, just like the Street trial, and it surely was tedious at times, but occasionally we were giddy when we remembered the high-stakes game of legal poker we were engaged in.

"YOU CAN MAKE THAT PHONE RING"

Meanwhile, ExxonMobil and its overpaid lawyers, their arrogance overflowing in the courtroom, were doing everything possible to lose the case. Their decision to have their corporate representative, Lindsay Booher, sit with their attorneys at the defense table was a bad idea in my opinion—further reminding the teachers, cops, and housewives of the jury that it was the wealth and hubris of Big Oil that was on trial. Remember, Booher—and his 1987 meeting with ITCO's Hooper—was actually central to our case, which meant that I got a chance to grill him on the witness stand.

On April 21, 2001, I confronted Booher with the company memos that showed ExxonMobil's forerunners had known about the radioactivity problems in the oil patch back in the early 1950s, yet had failed to act in a way to protect the people who were continually exposed to radioactive materials.

"When was the first time you checked your oil wells in Louisiana for radioactivity?" I asked the ExxonMobil hygienist.

"The first time I checked?"

"The first time Exxon checked, Mr. Booher."

"I'm not sure of the exact date we checked. I know we were checking in the '70s. We were finding radon to ensure that the other materials weren't being produced like radium-226. I couldn't tell you the specific first date. I assume from this memo somebody checked in '51 or '52."

"You presume...?"

"I didn't say 'presume,' I said I assume that somebody checked in '51 or '52 based on advice of Dr. Eckert," Booher said, referencing the oil company's chief medical officer who wrote the memo.

"Mr. Booher, you have absolutely no evidence that they checked on anything?"

"When?"

"In 1951."

"No, I don't."

"You don't have any evidence or document showing they did absolutely anything about the radioactivity coming out of the oil wells until 1986, correct?"

"Let me finish. I don't believe we discovered it coming out, radium-226, from our wells in the U.S. until 1986," Booher responded.

"Exactly. So obviously nobody followed the advice of this person in the memo to go check your wells, right?"

"I don't agree with that."

"Naturally not."

On the very afternoon that I was grilling Lindsay Booher on the stand, ExxonMobil was revealing its profits for the first quarter of 2001: $5 billion, in just three months. The next day we were back at it in the courthouse on Loyola Avenue. Under my questioning, Booher gave damaging testimony. For example, he acknowledged that ExxonMobil had done nothing, not even in 1986 when the TERM crisis went public, to inventory and track down all that old pipe that was lined with highly radioactive scale, pipe that sometimes ended up in schools or public playgrounds. Then we went on to the issue of worker safety at the Harvey yard during the 1990s.

"You found out in 1986 that there was radium-226 in some of your pipe yards, or '87, right?" I asked.

"They weren't our pipe yards but there was—was pipe—radium-226 in pipe yards."

"Pipe yards where you sent equipment to have cleaned, right?"

"Yes."

"Did you or Exxon perform any investigation at all as to whether any of the workers at your pipe yards or any of the members of the public that lived around your pipe yards may have been adversely affected by Exxon's radioactive waste, sir?"

Lindsay Booher, ExxonMobil's industrial hygienist, looked at me and the jury in silence. There was nothing he could say. The richest company on Earth had known it was harming these workers, and yet it did nothing. It was a law-school textbook case of willful, wanton behavior and gross negligence. In the end, I did battle with Booher for three days, pitting my self-taught expertise against Booher's training at the prestigious Massachusetts Institute of Technology.

I explained to jurors how ExxonMobil had perpetrated a "big lie" after 1986 by continuing to insist that the oil-patch pipe that it shipped to yards like ITCO was tested and shown not to be radioactive. The problems were twofold: Pipe was considered OK for delivery even if the tests showed radiation was four-times higher than background. More importantly, the readings were taken outside the pipe even though that radioactive scale that posed a lethal risk to the workers at ITCO was on the inside. Booher and I did battle for hours over this fallacy; I risked alienating jurors at times with my pointed lines of inquiry, and some of my colleagues urged me to cut it short, but at the end of the last day, Booher broke down, trying to defend a procedure that was indefensible, aimed at protecting ExxonMobil's hide, not the workers.

Knowing the stakes, our legal team had taken the extra step of hiring a shadow jury—citizens who we paid to sit in on the trial by day and share their thoughts with us in a hotel conference room at night. (ITCO, which was also a defendant in the case, but whose lawyers—like us—were looking to pin the entire problem on ExxonMobil, was doing the same thing.) It was like a prizefight in which we knew the judges had us way ahead on points. The shadow jurors said they would award us at least a half-billion dollars, and their numbers kept going higher as the trial wore on.

The pressure was on ExxonMobil and its attorneys to avoid a catastrophe, but somehow they weren't seeing what everyone else was seeing inside Judge Gill-Jefferson's courtroom. Mike later described the oil company's approach both down in Harvey and now inside the courtroom as "scorched earth tactics"—a consistent valuing of profits over people and a blind spot to both the short- and long-term consequences of that philosophy. After Booher's implosion on the witness stand, and with the shadow juries moving solidly to our side, I ran into an ExxonMobil corporate lawyer sent down from Houston to monitor the case in the courtroom one morning.

"What are you guys going to do?" I asked him. "You're losing this case. You're getting slaughtered."

"We're not paying more than single digits," he responded, brusquely. I was flabbergasted. ExxonMobil still thought they could get out of this mess for under $10 million. Talk about tunnel vision.

Instead, the self-delusional lawyers for the oil giant had one last move up their sleeve. They wanted to load the jurors on a bus, cross the high-arching Mississippi River bridge and take them on a tour of Harvey and the weedy, abandoned Grefer property. Their logic was simple. They simply assumed that when the jurors actually saw the ITCO site, its rusty, industrialized surroundings down by the canal, and the run-down community on the other side, the panel would realize that all this talk of $83 million to clean up such an inconsequential piece of land was ridiculous.

We put up a strenuous and vocal objection to their request, but in reality we were playing reverse psychology and mind games with ExxonMobil's overpriced attorneys. The more we were against it, the more they were for it. The truth was that we knew that the other side was making a huge miscalculation. The regular folks that we'd empanelled on the jury, all school teachers, city cops, and house-wives, grew up in and maybe even still lived in neighborhoods like the one they were about to see, and understood life in a working-class community over on the Westbank of the Mississippi in a way that completely eluded ExxonMobil's well-off attorneys.

Even so, we didn't want to take any chances. The radioactive con-tamination at the ITCO site was well-known in the community by 2001, especially after warning signs with the atomic symbol appeared on the property's fencing, telling the neighborhood kids not to play there. And so as word spread of our lawsuit against ExxonMobil, about a half-dozen families in Harvey who lived right next to the Grefer site had contacted us and said they were also interested in tak-ing legal action, if our claim proved successful. Some of the neigh-bors were also in court monitoring the trial.

But as happened throughout the Grefer case, we were also blessed with good luck. With our team squabbling with the ExxonMobil lawyers over the route, Judge Jefferson-Gill decided that she would determine the route—but when the appointed day came, the judge and her juror passengers got hopelessly lost.

Ultimately, the bus meandered toward the site from 16th Street, a quiet street of well-kept yards shaded by magnolia trees, a leafy one-way drive straight up to a radioactive warning gate. Their route would take them past the chalked playground and the sturdy faded brick of the St. Ville Academy, and in the shadow of the simple bone-white steeple of the New Testament Bible Baptist Center. As they cut south down Pailet Street, they passed modest but well-kept homes with vegetable gardens in the back and American flags in the shade of small palmettos and towering oaks. It proved to jurors that Harvey was a real place where middle-class families lived real lives, and that

ExxonMobil was trying to cut and run after dropping its own version of the atom bomb in the heart of town.

Frankly, we won the case that day, or at least we clinched the victory that was already at hand. Our legal team felt strongly that the testimony had clearly established the callousness of ExxonMobil in exposing its workers and the surrounding community to radioactive dust, but we still needed to wrap the package in a bow for the jury. Our expert, Stan Waligora, told the jurors that rather than the half-assed cleanup that ExxonMobil had suggested would cost $46,000, a serious cleanup, which would involve scraping the top two feet of soil off the entire parcel, and sifting through the dirt to make sure the radioactive hot spots were sent to a proper landfill, would cost $83 million. And what of the punitive damages? Jurors would need to decide how to get their message through to the ExxonMobil boardroom.

Once again, it was up to Jack to bring it all home. Clearly, Jack felt that some of the bruising battles at the witness box—especially my grueling three-day examination of Lindsay Booher—couldn't be ignored. We didn't want the jury to begin its deliberation with any ill feelings, especially not toward me.

"I'm going to ask you, also, to forgive my partner over there, Mr. Smith, OK?" Jack pleaded. "He's been an environmental lawyer for as long as I've known him, and he fights for little people and little communities against big companies for a very long time. I know his battles have some very deep scars and he fights pretty hard. Maybe I can teach him to be a little bit easier sometimes. But his phone number is 593-9600. If you've got something to tell him, go ahead and give him a call."

That got a small chuckle (although I can report that no one actually called), but Jack turned serious when he called on the jury to take advantage of this rare moment when regular folks suddenly had a level playing field with the titans of Big Oil.

He told them that "you are...the conscience of the community, and remember that by your decision you are going to set the standard...by which companies like ExxonMobil, nationwide, are going to have to behave. You are the verdict to correct a wrong that's been done to a community and to a people. You, by your verdict, can send a message to [ExxonMobil CEO Lee Raymond]. You, ladies and gentlemen, can get that phone call in his office. You have more power in your hands today than the heads of most Fortune 500 companies have. You can make that phone ring."

To empower the jury to award billions, Jack used an incredibly effective analogy. He took out eighty pennies and told the jury that each penny represented $1 billion of ExxonMobil's net worth of $80 billion. He got out a table with a white tablecloth in front of the jury and said, "You see that pile of pennies? That's ExxonMobil's net worth. If you decide to punish them, what's it going to take?" He swiped a penny away from the pile and said, "That's one billion...does that pile look any different?" Of course it did not. He then swiped two more and said the pile looks the same, but $3 billion will make them pay attention.

We were also very concerned about the jurors potentially making a mistake in the number of zeros on the verdict form. If we were going to get a big number, a missing "0" or an extra "0" could have been huge. Jack very carefully suggested they should forget about zeros and write the verdict out like a check—"three billion dollars."

Apparently they were listening to his advice.

The jury deliberated for one day and into a second. All of us knew it was going to be good news, but there was an air of unreality when we finally received the word that the verdict was in. Ron and Mike were eating lunch together when they were summoned back to Judge Gill-Jefferson's courthouse. They were jogging, sweating in their suits in the hot New Orleans spring, laughing out loud even as

Stuart and his team celebrating after the Grefer verdict.

their hearts were pounding. I wasn't laughing. "Where the hell have you been?!" I barked.

The next few minutes were surreal. The jury placed all of the financial responsibility onto ExxonMobil; they were assessed $56 million—more than four times what we'd told the company's lawyers we'd accept before the trial—for the cost of cleaning up the Grefer's property, and another $125,000 for the lost value of the property. Finally came the punitive damages.

It was written out on the verdict sheet, just as Jack had asked. "One billion dollars."

"You could have heard a pin drop," Mike Stag recalls of the moment. The lawyers for ExxonMobil looked sick to their stomach.

It was one thing to ask for $3 billion, but hearing the actual $1 billion verdict was mind-numbing. That night, April 22, 2001, we gathered on the balcony of my house in the French Quarter and threw a big party—me and Barry and Jack and Ron and Mike Stag and the whole trial team—and toasted our success with champagne. I still have the framed photo in a prominent place in my home. The Grefer verdict was another life-changing day for me.

And there had been so many thoughts that went through our minds at that remarkable moment. For a few hours, we would try to forget the reality that ExxonMobil was going to fight like hell, through Louisiana's notoriously conservative appeals courts, to get the $1.056 billion verdict thrown out, if not substantially reduced.

There were certainly thoughts about the workers, about Milton Vercher, who testified during the trial about working at ITCO but who wasn't allowed to mention his leukemia and his other ailments. Remarkably, he hung on for another eight years before passing away in 2009. But we were able to obtain justice for him and his family, and we took on the cases of other ITCO workers who'd been poisoned by the carelessness of the world's biggest and richest oil company.

Thanks in good measure to what happened inside that courtroom, we were able to win a $15 million jury verdict four years later on behalf of the wife and son of Lee Dell Craft, a longtime ITCO worker who died of lung cancer in 1986, before he or his co-workers even learned about the radioactivity at the site. There was something remarkable about the Craft case: We were able to establish that working on ExxonMobil's tainted pipes made them liable for his lung cancer, even though Craft was also a lifelong, two-pack-a-day smoker.

Indeed, there were certainly thoughts of justice, about how fighting for the little guy and winning is the reason we'd gotten into this racket in the first place—and now we'd taken that to the max. It's something that I don't always articulate well, and my colleague Ron said it better when I asked him about it recently. He said: "Part of it was ego, but part of it was, 'Here's a victory for common man'— because so often those voices are lost because you can't compete with the money, you can't compete with the power ... Goliath lawyers fight because they're just billing the hell out of their clients in most cases. For us, it's personal—we're trying to right a wrong."

Something that's even harder to put into words was the powerful sense of vindication. For nearly a decade, Big Oil had used every weapon in its massive arsenal to try to minimize what we'd accomplished in Hattiesburg: to minimize the significant health risk from its radioactive waste and the economic risk for the exposure of decades of reckless behavior. And it looked like they'd won a near total victory... until we heard those words, $1 billion. Now, other lawyers were looking to cash in on the foundation that we had set for them. In Louisiana, pollution lawsuits became a huge risk for the oil giants in the 2000s and beyond... and deservedly so. But that wouldn't have happened if we had not developed the Grefer case and rolled the dice in court. As my partner Mike Stag told me recently: "They almost got away with it."

I think such thoughts, too, but frankly, in a trial like the Grefer case I get caught up in the moment. I guess I'm just too competitive.

As we filed out of the courtroom, I walked past ExxonMobil's corporate lawyer monitoring the trial.

"You got your single digit now. One billion." He looked sick to his stomach.

SEVEN

THE FIRE THIS TIME

IN 1997, BARRY AND I finally bought a home together. It seemed like a long time, but it had only been five years since those long nights in the woods near Lake Geiger outside of Hattiesburg, hiding from the eviction notices under our door in suburban Metairie. In just a handful of years, I'd built a steady practice in environmental law, anchored by my expertise in oil-industry radiation cases, and Barry was now a practicing attorney as well. We could have lived a comfortably bland existence in the New Orleans suburbs, but neither of us wanted that lifestyle, not with the ornate, bright-hued splendor of the French Quarter within walking distance of our law offices. A stone's throw (what an ironic term) from the French Market, we found a historic, rambling 5,000-square-foot home, with a big old wooden door that opened onto a stone courtyard with a babbling fountain, a safe haven from the raucous Big Easy night.

Or so we thought. We'd only been in our new home for a little over a year when my mom, Judy, had moved in with us. On this late summer's night, her calm was broken by the sound of shattering glass and a frightening flash of orange light. She ran out to the courtyard to find a fire in the rear servants' quarters. Our home in the French Quarter had been firebombed—and not for the first time, either. Someone had hurled a Molotov cocktail over the rear roof and into our courtyard. I was at a deposition in Dallas in the Brookhaven case when I found out. I left immediately for New Orleans.

Barry and I hurried home to comfort Mom and to speak with the cops. They wanted to know, obviously, if Barry or I had any enemies. I laughed nervously, thinking of all the Big Oil companies I'd taken down in my years practicing law. It seemed crazy to think that any one of the energy giants that we'd battled in court was to blame, but I wasn't that far removed from the paranoid days of Paul Johnson State Park and that RV with all the antennas. Or maybe the firebomb was just some random craziness from the streets of the Crescent City.

It had started earlier with a Molotov cocktail that came out of nowhere and shattered on our front balcony, but which thankfully didn't do any significant damage to our home. It was just six nights later that we were urgently summoned outside. This time it was Barry's Mercedes-Benz, a law-school graduation gift from me, that was consumed in flames; in a few short minutes, it was burned beyond repair. Another Molotov cocktail had been hurled, this time through a broken window in the rear door. The good news was that no one was hurt...so far. If this mad firebomber intended to scare us away from the French Quarter, these attacks had only stiffened our resolve to stay put. And we needed every ounce of that resolve.

The Vieux Carré had become our own personal war zone—and we'd been there for a little over a year. It was a time of both fear and frustration, and we began to question if the New Orleans police shared our urgency in finding the culprit. In January 1998, fed up with the lack of progress or even interest in the case from the local authorities, I held a public press conference to decry the pace of the investigation. It was not long after that the Bureau of Alcohol, Tobacco, and Firearms got involved, but even ATF was stymied at first.

Six months later, the Saturn that I'd purchased for Barry to replace the Mercedes was also set on fire out in the street. Ironically, I'd purchased an economy car this time because this was exactly what I had feared would happen. I was sorry to be right. Meanwhile, I was still worried that the chickens were coming home to roost—specifically, my increasingly high profile as a public enemy of Big Oil. I kept thinking of the story that Clark Street had told me up in Laurel a few years back, how someone had shot up his car because he was asking too many questions out in the oil patch. In the late 1990s, I was doing a lot of oil litigation work in places like the rugged foothills of eastern Kentucky. Hatfield versus McCoy country, right? Was someone now trying to send me a message?

Although it went against every instinct in my body, by now I was actually considering moving. Then, finally, after seventeen long months and posting an extraordinary reward of $15,000, the feds announced not one but two arrests. And it turned out that Big Oil had nothing to do with it.

The firebombers were the owner of a nightclub around the corner called the Gazebo Restaurant and Bar, a man by the name of George Mellen Jr., and his accomplice Richard "the Chicken Man" Jones. Federal prosecutors uncovered that Mellen was giving cash and even free food to Jones to lob the Molotov cocktails at our home and our car in an effort to intimidate us.

The motive? We'd been lodging increasingly aggressive noise complaints about the Gazebo on behalf of a neighbor with whom we had become close friends. When we moved onto our picturesque new side street, we were shocked to learn that Mellen's club—and a couple of others—were offering loud live music without any of the proper permits, making a racket that kept our new neighbors awake until the early morning hours. It turned out that clubs like the Gazebo had been violating the New Orleans noise ordinance for years, to the point that French Quarter residents had grown tired of fighting back. But we weren't.

We formed alliances with some of our neighbors, and volunteered our talents as litigation lawyers pro bono. We went into court and sued the Gazebo for not having a music license. Apparently the owner wasn't used to someone challenging the way he did business, and so he thought that a couple of well-timed firebombs would scare us away and that, as usual, nothing would happen to him as a consequence. And he almost got away with it. But he didn't know me, didn't know that I'd already taken on oil companies worth hundreds of billions of dollars. I wasn't going to be intimidated by some pissant, small-time bar owner. I was the only lawyer I had ever heard of to be firebombed for taking a pro bono case. Mellen was caught on tape by the Chicken Man, who was wearing a wire after being fingered for the reward by a friend who then skipped town. Mellen was heard on tape saying, "I want you to get the big black Mercedes— that will make the front page of the *Times-Picayune*." He was referring to my safely garaged SL.

The arrest of George Mellen and the Chicken Man marked the beginning of a new chapter for me. Much as I'd done a decade earlier, when I hit the books in order to do battle with the nation's radiation authorities, I now resolved to become an expert on the problem of noise pollution. The situation was very analogous to what had happened in the oil patch, in that years of unchecked pollution had taken a toll. Population data showed that the number of people living in the French Quarter had plummeted, from more than 12,000 folks at the start of the 1970s to barely 3,000 at the turn of the millennium, and you didn't need to be Perry Mason to resolve the case of why. When the oil economy hit rock bottom, city officials had turned to tourism to survive, and were content to turn the priceless Vieux Carré into a Disneyland-with-booze to lure in young, free-spending partiers, local residents be damned. The mayor at the time, Marc Morial, admitted as much when he told the newspapers that "[a] lot of what the complaining is about really has to do with the comeback of the entire city."

Don't call it a comeback. Working with a coalition of resident groups determined to save what was left of the French Quarter, we argued that smart code enforcement would protect all the important live music venues and only target the real nuisance bars or itinerant street musicians who didn't think twice about playing amped-up tunes under someone's window at 3 a.m. Over time, we helped launch a campaign called "Hear the Music, Stop the Noise," which became a leading umbrella coalition of groups who pressed the city to simply start enforcing its noise ordinance and its zoning laws that were already on the books.

In doing so, I managed to make a few new enemies—and a ton of great new friends. One of my proudest public moments came in the spring of 2012 when I was awarded the Elizebeth T. Werlein Medal by the Vieux Carré Commission for the pro bono work I'd done on behalf of the neighborhood I came to consider our home. My involvement in the New Orleans noise-pollution fight epitomized my increasingly rich and complex life as I moved toward middle age. My eighteen-hour days and subsequent success as an environmental attorney gave me wealth and some freedom to pursue other interests, but whatever I took on, I did it my way—head down, full steam ahead. My personal life is a source of great satisfaction—just don't call it leisure time, because there's not much sitting.

Indeed, my life began to change dramatically in the mid-2000s. We knew that ExxonMobil was going to fight with everything it had to get the $1 billion damages in the Grefer case tossed out. Heck, we knew the dollar figure would probably get knocked down. But we had done too much to establish reckless negligence by ExxonMobil for even Louisiana's appeals-court judges to ignore. Although the higher court did reduce the amount of punitive damages imposed on ExxonMobil, Louisiana's 4th Circuit Court of Appeals let stand both the verdict and a substantial penalty that amounted, with interest, to more than $200 million. And it did so with some of the most withering language that I have seen in an environmental case. The justices ruled that the oil giant was guilty of "callous, calculated, despicable, and reprehensible conduct" in its years of dumping on the Grefer property and poisoning the workers there. "The fact that Exxon showed no regard for worker safety certainly demonstrates that it had even less concern for the property damage that it caused, thus further demonstrating the morally culpable nature of its conduct," the court wrote in its blistering sixty-one-page opinion, which found that ExxonMobil officials had intentionally withheld information that could have protected the health and safety of the workers at ITCO.

The final verdict on ExxonMobil had a powerful impact on me. For nearly two decades, I'd been a raging bull, fueled both by my sense of injustice and my equally strong desire for personal success. Now, that big check from the world's richest oil company allowed me to catch my breath, to pursue other passions in life, many of them outside of a courtroom or a law library. I had also done well enough that I could start giving back, through pro bono legal work on neighborhood issues in the French Quarter and by becoming a major political donor, not only in local races but to the national Democratic Party and related progressive causes. In July 2008, I pledged funds to Loyola University to support its law clinic—now known as the Stuart H. Smith Law Clinic and Center for Social Justice—and to endow a professorship in the name of my mentor, the late Jack Nelson, a longtime Loyola professor and leader in civil rights and poverty law.

Stuart on one of his trips around the world.

As I approached fifty, maybe a part of me was thinking about training the next generation because I was taking this step back. The obsessive qualities that I once brought to learning radiation law I now brought to my new hobbies in life. Barry and I purchased an Oyster yacht, the Pandemonium, and we cruised the planet, from the Caribbean to the waters off Croatia to an around-the-world rally in 2013. Our global sailing runs also allowed us to take advantage of our love of scuba diving, as we explored the Great Barrier Reef and other remarkable worlds that exist below the surface. Our arrival on Pandemonium was announced with a large cruising gennaker bearing art in the 1980s Pop Shop style of our favorite artist, the late Keith Haring, whose art also lined the walls of our home back in the French Quarter.

The quest for new worlds to conquer and the disruption of Hurricane Katrina even encouraged us to establish a second homestead, a glistening condo at the very southern tip of Miami's South Beach, with a wraparound balcony that looked out on the warm aqua-blue waters of the South Atlantic. Both as a hobby and to connect our two homes, Barry and I got our pilot licenses and bought a TBM 850, a sleek single-engine turboprop that's used to train French fighter pilots. The TBM 850 can hit a top speed of about 345 mph, and when it does, it just sips gasoline compared to a normal jet. At those moments, the plane is about as fuel efficient as a Hummer barreling down the interstate at 65 mph. But that's excellent mileage at 320 miles an hour.

OK, I know what you're probably thinking right now. Shouldn't an environmental crusader be a little more...carbon-neutral? Look, there are some folks out there who fight pollution in the manner of Henry David Thoreau, from their solar-paneled log cabin by a pond way back in the woods, but I'm not that guy. The reason I am Big Oil's worst nightmare is because I know how to hit them in the one place where it causes real pain—in the wallet. I get justice by taking money, a lot of money, from the polluters and poisoners and getting it for the everyday folks who are my clients...and for myself. You may not find that the ideal way, but it's really the only way to fight the oil companies in the twenty-first century—crude justice.

Put another way: There's a term in a law that describes what happens when companies profit by breaking the law or committing acts of gross negligence: "unjust enrichment." I got a lot of money back for folks like the Streets, dumped on in the woods of south-central Mississippi, and the relatives of Lee Dell Craft, the working-class African-American worker who died of lung cancer after toiling in radioactive scale for decades—and I got paid as well.

I call this "just enrichment."

And so by the start of a new decade, 2010, I was living the life I had always wanted to live—that of a high-flying (literally), successful American tort lawyer. We can be the Jedi knights of the justice system: feisty and argumentative, flamboyant, a bit larger-than-life at times. After defeating ExxonMobil in court, however, I concentrated on cases that really mattered to me. This included working with my home state's top activist group, the Louisiana Environmental Action Network, or LEAN, on a case to stop offshore oil drillers from dumping radioactive water right back into the Gulf of Mexico. But at times by 2010 I took to describing myself, at the age of just forty-eight, as in a state of semi-retirement.

I should have known better with Big Oil. Michael Corleone said it best: "Just when I thought I was out, they pull me back in."

"THERE'S A HUGE FIRE IN THE GULF"

Wednesday, April 21, 2010, was a beautiful morning in the southern United States—warm, sun-drenched, perfect for flying. Barry and I were up early, taking off from the airport north of Miami around 6:30 a.m. I was headed back to New Orleans for some more work on our radiation disposal case with LEAN. Truth be told, I might have easily forgotten all about the flight—Barry and I had cruised this route high above the swampy Everglades, the beachfront condos of St. Petersburg, and the azure Gulf waters dozens of times. It was so routine that I often had to remind myself of something that the first flight instructor who trained Barry and me had said: When flying a single-engine plane you always had to stay a little on edge.

That was good advice. On this Wednesday morning, Barry and I would see something that we'd never seen before.

The radio was tuned to New Orleans air traffic control as we closed in on the Lakefront airport. When we were nearing Red Fin waypoint, an anchored buoy with a radio beacon, we heard air traffic control instructing another private plane pilot. This, too, was routine—until the pilot started to repeat back the command.

"Seven-eight-three Echo Foxtrot, clear direct Red Fin direct Harvey for a visual approach on Three-six left—Holy Shit! There's a huge fire in the Gulf!"

"It's a fire on an oil rig," air traffic control said. "We just heard about it, and we're vectoring traffic around it."

Ten minutes later, Barry and I could see the fire. Even at a distance of more than a hundred miles, as close as we got before our own approach into New Orleans Lakefront airport, the fire shocked and awed us. It looked like a giant blowtorch, flames as bright as the sun shooting up and out from a drilling platform obscured by billowing black smoke.

"I hope to God they got everyone off that thing safely," I said.

"Amen," Barry replied.

But by the time I reached my law office on the twenty-eighth floor of a 1990s-era skyscraper at the edge of the French Quarter that looked out on the wide expanse of the Mississippi River, reports were streaming in, and the news was not at all good. We learned that the rig was British Petroleum's *Deepwater Horizon*. Although that didn't immediately mean anything to the general public, those of us in the Louisiana environmental community were quite familiar with the project. That was because of the size and audacity of the BP endeavor—drilling in a mile's depth of open water—and the company's insistence of having implemented unprecedented safety measures.

The *Deepwater Horizon* was yet another indicator of how the energy game had changed since I started suing oil companies at the end of the 1980s. With crude oil often selling for as much as $100 a barrel or more, the heavyweights like BP, Shell, and ExxonMobil were exploring at literally the ends of the earth—miles out in the Gulf, or in the Arctic Ocean, or with a new process called "fracking" that involved injecting chemicals to break up shale formations deep under the earth. Big Oil was eager for the rewards of what some called "extreme drilling," yet there'd been such little talk of the enormous risks.

Now the nightmare scenario was unfolding right in my backyard, off the coast of my native Louisiana. It turned out that the intense fire that Barry and I had seen from the air was from a sudden explosion that had happened the night before. There was talk of many workers from the *Deepwater Horizon* missing and feared dead. Working on an offshore oil rig—which was an economic lifeline for thousands of blue-collar workers up and down the Gulf Coast during the 1970s and 1980s—had always been one of the most dangerous jobs around, as I'd learned handling injury cases earlier in my career. I'd visited clients over the years who'd been burned in fires like the one that we had witnessed that morning—victims who were completely covered in bandages and in excruciating pain from third-degree burns from head to foot, who wished they hadn't survived. But still no one is prepared for a tragedy of this magnitude.

"I've got a bad feeling about it," Marylee Orr, the founder and longtime executive director of LEAN, told me on the speakerphone that first crazy morning, during our scheduled call on the radioactive dumping lawsuit. "I'm hearing on the grapevine that BP won't let the rig workers' families know anything. They can't find out who's alive, injured, or what."

That sounded typical: Big Oil trying to get its story straight. Immediately, my antenna went up for the kind of behavior that I'd seen before. The rest of America was just absorbing the headline news on cable TV, that a rescue mission was underway in the Gulf for a dozen or so men. But I was already thinking ahead, to the environmental catastrophe that might come next. Did BP or anyone else even know how to plug up a leaking wellhead one mile under the surface? And I knew from all my past experiences that the British oil giant would probably try to minimize estimates of any oil spill, and that the firm probably wouldn't be

above doubling-down on the health and safety risks to any workers it hired to clean up its mess.

We would soon learn that eleven men perished in the explosion
on the rig that occurred on the night of April 20, 2010—men who
in many cases had left a wife or their children onshore to try to earn
a bigger paycheck, and who would never come home. It would take
longer to learn the other truths that were so unsurprising to anyone
who has followed Big Oil and its safety track record.

I knew within the first couple of days that the causes of the BP
tragedy would be thoroughly investigated, but that the immediate
ongoing crisis was oil leaking from the damaged wellhead. I was
working closely with a young attorney in my firm who had a petroleum engineering degree to monitor the Internet sites where experts
talk to one another, and so we knew that the damaged rig had sunk
even before it was reported on CNN. But, at first, we had no information to counter the oil company claims that 8,000 barrels of oil
per day were leaking from the site—a significant number, but not
catastrophic.

Three days after the explosion, I watched an exclusive interview with Coast Guard Rear Admiral Mary Landry on local station
WDSUH. She was the government's initial point person on the spill.
"We've got 24/7 remote video at the wellhead, and there is no oil
leaking from the wellhead or the riser," she said. The admiral added
that industry and government had both learned their lessons from
the Exxon Valdez disaster in 1989. There were "robust resources" in
place, she added, to clean up the relatively small oil slick left over
from the explosion, and crews would be "forward leaning" if further
trouble arose.

That was reassuring news. I assumed—mistakenly, of course—
that the blowout preventer was working. But then the next day there
were reports in the local media that in fact the blowout preventer
had failed and oil was leaking, but at the modest rate of 1,000 barrels

a day. Things were not adding up. The leak had gone from 8,000 barrels to zero to 1,000 barrels in little more than two days? What I also didn't know then was that the video that BP was showing to the Coast Guard's Landry wasn't really the leaking wellhead.

On Sunday, April 25, I was up early and obsessing over the BP situation, scrolling the Internet for any news I could find. A Web site with the highly appropriate name of Skytruth.org showed satellite photos revealing that an oil spill was already covering 400 square miles of the Gulf. I couldn't believe it! The leak had to be much, much larger than BP and the Coast Guard were telling the citizenry. I texted my associate and he called me back five minutes later.

"Oil's got to be gushing out of that wellhead," he told me.

"One thing we know for sure," I said. "It's not 1,000 barrels per day or anything close to that."

That moment confirmed the gut instinct that I'd had the moment that Barry and I had first seen the fire from the air—that my life for the time being wasn't going to be the same, that if I had in fact been moving toward semi-retirement, I certainly wasn't anymore. A completely uncontrolled leak would require the drilling of a relief well—a massive project that would take at least three months. And based on production numbers from a similar BP well, a leak of this kind could be as much as 60,000 barrels a day, maybe even 120,000 barrels a day during that time.

I had already put the firm on alert and began calling toxic tort lawyer friends from around the Gulf Coast to put together a team to handle the case, convinced that if the spill worsened we'd get a flood of calls from fishermen and others seeking to pursue claims against one of the world's richest oil companies. I also expected a ton of media calls. We certainly had a unique role to play. Most folks in New Orleans were trained to trust authority, to believe what the oil companies and the government had to say. We were the doubters, the skeptics. Even we didn't realize how important that would become.

Indeed, over the next few days, as anecdotal evidence spread that a major disaster was underway in the Gulf, the Coast Guard continued to rely on faulty estimates supplied by interested officials from BP, thus misleading the public on the extent of the spill. Some ten days after the explosion, the government continued to publicize an estimate that only 5,000 barrels (or 275,000 gallons) a day were surging from the exploded rig. Clearly, executives from the British firm were hoping to head off a complete PR disaster while they tried to come up with a plan to cap the well. In addition, the penalties that they'd ultimately be assessed under the Clean Water Act would be based on the size of the spill, so billions of dollars were at stake with the estimates.

"In the environmental arena, human health risk modeling is done day in and day out for every type of pollutant, whether going in the water, earth, or air," I said in a statement that was released to the media that week. "Why are BP and the Environmental Protection Agency not releasing such information to the public?"

A few days later, the national media was now descending on New Orleans as the Deepwater Horizon disaster became a top-of-the-hour breaking news story. I flew with CNN reporter Ed Lavandera and his film crew in the TBM to get an aerial view of the fast-spreading slick. While we were aloft, I had the chance to speak to a national TV audience that was suddenly interested in the battle that I'd been waging against Big Oil for twenty years. We spoke of how the federal government—in granting a permit to BP to drill in such deep water off Louisiana—was way too trusting of BP's assurances that a spill was unlikely, to the point where the federal agency then known as the Minerals Management Service (MMS) had waived a more stringent environmental review.

"Once you dig into it, I mean, they are treated with kid gloves in every respect," I told the CNN reporter. "They are the least-regulated industry from an environmental point of view in the country."

"Obviously, they're going to argue just the opposite," Lavandera responded.

"Well, they can't."

If I sounded a bit brusque, maybe that's because part of me was amazed that the nation was just now catching on to the things that I had seen for so long—that Big Oil had both the politicians and the regulators who work for them in their back pocket, that profits had long been valued over worker safety, and that no one paid much attention to any of this until eleven good men lost their lives and the Gulf of Mexico became the world's largest petroleum tank.

On the surface, the Deepwater Horizon catastrophe was a completely new and different chapter for us. For two decades, my partners and I had carved out a tight but critically important specialty in uncovering the radiological pollution caused by the oil giants and recovering damages on behalf of the victims. Big offshore oil spills were new for us. But the reality was that our real specialty was getting inside of Big Oil's head. We knew their tricks. We knew that just as the oil company lawyers had perfected "dose dancing" on radiation, BP was sure to fudge, obfuscate, and flat-out lie about how much oil was leaking from the rig. We knew that whenever there was a choice between protecting workers and the environment or saving a few bucks, that BP would go with cutting corners. In many ways, my entire career had been building to take on the British energy giant, but this battle would be fought on very different turf: less before a judge than before the court of public opinion.

That was the big picture, but there wasn't much time to think about it.

"I KNOW THAT I'M GOING TO DIE..."

Just as I had expected, the phone was ringing off the hook in our law offices up on the twenty-eighth floor. Many of the calls were coming from Gulf Coast fisherman who knew of our past environmental work. Life is never easy for these hearty souls who know not only the exhilaration of returning to port with a net full of the Gulf's bounty, but also the frustration of a dead sea, the increasing result of runoff and man-made pollution. But they'd never experienced an emotional roller-coaster ride like those hectic first days after the spill. The authorities had moved quickly to shut down fishing in the pollution zone, understandably, but now here was BP offering to hire the fleet captains and their crews for cleanup work, at a decent rate of pay—as much as $2,000 a day for bigger boats. It was ironic that you had to go to work for the company responsible for taking away everything you hold dear in order to put food on the table. And to get the work that the oil company was offering—the only work that was available—the fishermen would need to sign something called a Master Charter Agreement.

Marylee recalled how fishermen first started coming to her, showing her the seventeen-page agreement that BP was asking them to sign. She quickly realized that coastal residents anxious for money to keep feeding their families in the wake of the oil spill were certain to sign the document without even reading it, even as they were potentially signing away their legal rights for a much larger payday down the road. "Some of our people who signed it did so under stress," she said. "You couldn't sue, you couldn't talk if your boat got damaged."

It was now May, and the first full week of the cleanup operation was coming to an end. BP and government experts and some of the world's smartest petro-chemical experts were frantically engaged in deliberations about how to deal with a blown wellhead under one mile of water, and officials were also still unable to agree on how much oil was spewing forth every day. Marylee Orr and George Barasich, the president of the Commercial Fishermen's Association, came to me with copies of the agreement and begged me to do something as soon as possible.

I was equally appalled by the seventeen-page document. Even though BP was 100 percent responsible for the oil spill and cleaning it up, the agreement sought to indemnify the oil company against any accident involving the boats they were hiring to clean it up. The profit-laden oil company wanted a free ride on the insurance policies of these volunteers, so it would be these middle-class working folks who would see their rates at risk if anything happened. BP also wanted a thirty-day notice if any of the cleanup workers were planning to sue the company, which most certainly were. Perhaps most alarmingly, BP wanted to strip the volunteers of their First Amendment rights by telling the signers they could not speak with others about what they had seen during the spill cleanup without the company's approval.

This was the weekend, but given the urgency of the around-the-clock cleanup, our team prepared and filed a request for an emergency injunction to at least nullify the most offensive portions of the agreement. On a Sunday afternoon, U.S. District Judge Ginger Berrigan opened up her courtroom to allow us to plead our case. After hearing our argument and BP's defense of the agreement, Judge Berrigan agreed with our argument that the restrictions were overly broad, and BP then agreed to stipulate that the contested passages were no longer in effect. It was the first victory for plaintiffs in what would be years of BP litigation.

With so much gloom over the future of the Gulf and the working people who depended on it, it was gratifying to beat BP in a legal skirmish; in a statement that afternoon I called it "an amazing example of how well our civil justice system works for the hard-working people of America, such as Louisiana fishermen who most need it right now."

But I knew the struggle was just beginning.

Maybe it was my experience fighting for folks like the Streets or the ITCO workers down in Harvey, but my thoughts had already turned to the cleanup workers, and what prolonged exposure to oil—which is laden with carcinogens like benzene—might do to them. I immediately began researching past spills that seemed most comparable to what was happening now at the Macondo oil field in the Gulf. I called people up in Alaska, where the 1989 wreck of the *Exxon Valdez* occurred. The massive cleanup that ensued was one of the few examples of what the Gulf cleanup workers might expect.

I also read up on a similar incident involving the Greek tanker *Tasman Spirit*, which had been carrying crude oil from Iran to Pakistan when it went aground near Karachi in July 2003, spilling more than 35,000 tons of oil into the sea and along seven miles of the highly populated residential and recreational coastline. The oil itself caused considerable damage to fish and wildlife outside the Pakistani city, but the worst damage to human health came through the air because an estimated 11,000 tons of volatile organic compounds (VOCs) were also released. Hospitals were flooded with people complaining of headaches, dizziness, and nausea.

Remarkably, no one was talking much about the threat of VOCs in the air along the Gulf Coast, even for cleanup workers who were traveling to the edge of the spill in boats and removing oil from the beaches. Based on what I called "back of the envelope" calculations, I estimated in early May 2010 that as much as ten times as many VOCs could go airborne off Louisiana as in the Pakistani disaster, or more than 100,000 tons. I consulted with a top toxicologist who would become a valuable ally, Dr. William Sawyer. He agreed that the greatest dangers from the Deepwater Horizon disaster would either come from breathing polluted air or from direct bodily contact with the oil. His grim forecast would prove prophetic.

This is why we were shocked to learn that the cleanup workers—hired by BP for a seafaring program it called, with no sense of irony, Vessels of Opportunity—and a growing number of beachfront volunteers were mostly tackling their jobs without serious protective gear.

Marylee recalled that she'd learned from our experts that it was absolutely critical for cleanup workers to wear protective clothing and use respirators to prevent breathing in the carcinogenic VOCs *after* she started getting back disturbing health reports from the Coast. Most of the workers she spoke with had been hired to attach oil-catching booms to their shrimp boats in place of nets and drive their boats directly through the oil slicks to corral and collect the oil that was spilling from BP's broken well. Others were on igniter boats, tasked with throwing devices that were like Molotov cocktails onto the oil in order to burn it off.

"We were hearing from our fishermen that they had headaches, vomiting, nausea, dizziness, and would get chest pains—and then they'd get on land and feel better," she said. "At first, we wondered if the opposition to proper safety gear was simply lack of knowledge among BP and the people running its cleanup operation. But quickly we began to suspect the reason was simply that BP and the federal officials monitoring its response to the spill were eager to convey a sense of normalcy, that there was no oil-spill crisis, and very soon it would be A-OK for tourists to return. BP knew that providing protective equipment would be an admission that the oil exposure was dangerous and sought to avoid this at all costs," Marylee said.

"My theory is the appearance—even when they were still cleaning the beaches, they were allowing people to come back. And you see a worker who's in a 'moon suit' or some other protective gear and you think maybe this is not a good place for me....The pressure to open the Gulf, to get people eating the seafood and people back in the condos was so great. They spent millions and millions of dollars advertising."

To put it as bluntly as I can, I believe BP cared more about its public image than if the fishermen of the Gulf got cancer. I have no "proof" of this, but this is what I believe.

At first, it was the wives who called, because their husbands were too proud, or too afraid of losing their income, to complain. It was only a few months later that Orr heard from a male worker who was involved in the beach cleanup. "He said, 'On the beach, I have seen children running away with brown stains on their feet because of the oil. I have already been airlifted out once [because of a medical emergency] and I know I'm going to die because of all the oil.' I thought he was an old man because of his voice. That's when he told me he was twenty-six."

That spring, LEAN explained the crisis to its best donors and raised $12,000 to buy protective gear—hundreds of half-face respirators and organic vapor cartridges, as well as nitrile gloves, sleeve protectors, and booties—to distribute free to some of the cleanup workers.

"There's no way you can be working in that toxic soup without getting exposure," Hugh Kaufman, a senior policy analyst at the EPA's office of solid waste and emergency response and a longtime whistleblower, told the *Washington Post*. It had been just a decade since he'd watched workers at the post-9/11 cleanup at the World Trade Center fall ill after not wearing respirators, and now it was happening all over again. "It's unbelievable what's going on. It's like deja vu."

At the height of the cleanup in late May, at least nine cleanup workers were hospitalized in one week, including seven who were taken to the hospital on May 26, 2010, after complaining of nausea, dizziness, and headaches. That prompted the Coast Guard to order all 125 boats working in the Breton Sound area to return to port as a precaution. It was one of the few times that any precautions were taken, frankly.

During this time, we were pursuing any and all legal means to force BP, the Coast Guard, and other agencies to require protective gear. Just as we had done with the other onerous stipulations in the Master Charter Agreement, we went into court, seeking a restraining order on behalf of the Gulf fishermen against the oil giant. Once again, we won...or so I thought. We gained a requirement that BP yet again rewrite the agreement to guarantee that cleanup workers receive proper hazardous materials, or haz-mat, training and be provided with all necessary safety gear at BP's expense. But this proved to be very much a Pyrrhic victory. BP took what you could call a minimalist approach to determining what constituted proper safety equipment. This included its determination that respirators—the one item that could have done the most good in protecting the workers both from short-term symptoms and the risk of cancer—were still not necessary. And the most galling part of it was that the federal government sided with BP in the matter.

In early June, two key Democratic members of Congress— Minnesota Representative James Oberstar, then-chairman of the House Transportation and Infrastructure Committee, and New York Representative Jerrold Nadler, a senior member of the committee— sent a letter to the EPA and the Department of Labor to express their alarm at learning what we'd known for weeks, that fishers and other cleanup workers were getting headaches and experiencing breathing difficulties. The powerful pols demanded that the Gulf workers be provided with "proper protective equipment, including respirators."

Incredibly, the Obama administration said "no" to this.

David Michaels, the assistant secretary of the Labor Department, who oversaw the Occupational Safety and Health Administration, or OSHA, told the *Wall Street Journal* that their tests showed "minimal" risk from exposure to airborne toxins. This, despite the fact that the

EPA's air monitors along the Gulf Coast were picking up substantial airborne VOC readings from the spill—which was centered fifty miles offshore—and despite scores of alarming medical reports from the actual workers.

Michaels, reported the *Journal* at the time, "remains worried about heat illnesses, given the high temperatures, long hours and resulting fatigue. He also is concerned about injuries 'because there are many hazards out there such as bites from wildlife, wet and slippery or uneven surfaces, boats and use of heavy equipment.'" Part of this is just the incredible myopia of government bureaucrats. These are the kind of people who get a lot more worried about a wobbly ladder than if the ladder was standing in a jet stream of pure benzene.

Over the course of a long, hot Louisiana summer, Marylee watched helplessly as unprotected fishermen and others kept going out to sea in their "Vessels of Opportunity" and came back into port feeling sick. "This whole thing has been very disillusioning for people," she said. "I had a government official tell me that if we pushed [BP] too hard, we will get stuck with the cleanup bill."

As for me, I'm a cynical soul by nature, but I have to confess that I had once had somewhat raised hopes for this administration; after all, I had gone to the convention in Denver and donated handsomely to the Democrats in the 2008 election cycle, eagerly hoping for the "change" in Washington that Obama had promised. Maybe when it came to BP, the White House had bigger fish to fry. Around the same time that the Labor Department was siding with BP over the respirators, Obama was on the phone to the British prime minister, David Cameron, who was in a tizzy because so many English pensioners had their retirement money tied up in BP stock.

"The president made clear that he had no interest in undermining BP's value," Cameron's office announced after the phone call. Really? Maybe Britain and its retirees should have invested in a more socially responsible fashion. There was no fine or legal judgment that would be enough, frankly, to punish BP's unjust enrichment, or to make sure another oil firm didn't behave as badly.

The truth that we were coming to learn about President Barack Obama is that the promised change agent, at least when it came to Big Oil, was really a wishy-washy compromiser. As oil spewed uninterrupted from the Macondo field into the Gulf, Obama took the unprecedented step of addressing the nation in a primetime television address, a sign that the BP crisis posed not just an environmental threat but a political one as well. On June 16, 2010, one month before the leaking well had been capped and the full extent of the damage could be investigated, the White House announced an unprecedented deal with BP in which the oil company would finance a relief fund of up to $20 billion.

"This is about accountability and at the end of the day, that's what every American wants and expects," Obama said in the State Dining Room that day. At the same time, BP executives made a pretense of apologizing profusely to the people of the Gulf. "Words are not enough," BP's chairman Carl Henric Svenberg said solemnly. "We will be judged by our actions."

On one level, Obama had maneuvered through a tight spot politically, trying to escape a bind that had been created by his predecessors, who just a generation earlier had lacked the imagination to anticipate a spill of the magnitude that BP had unleashed on the Gulf or how the profits raked in by the world's biggest oil companies would grow from mega-millions to mega-billions. In the wake of the 1989 Alaska spill—which was terrible but paled in comparison to the Deepwater Horizon catastrophe—Congress had passed a measure that required oil companies to pay all costs for cleaning up spills, but limited their potential damages to a mere $75 million. That would come nowhere near compensating the Gulf fishers, charter boat captains, or seafood processors who faced the prospect of losing their income for at least months, maybe even years.

The escrow fund, if nothing else, was good politics—$20 billion was a number that sure sounded impressive to the average voter but would prove to be music to the ears of the board members of BP, and all those retirees in Leeds and Newcastle that David Cameron was trying to protect. The history of such escrow funds is that they furnish an effective way for companies to limit their liability. They are a tool for persuading vulnerable people in desperate need to sign away their legal rights to recover full compensation for the damages they've suffered. When Big Oil's political allies vilify the escrow fund as "a shakedown," they're just helping the deception along by crying foul. Twenty years after the Exxon Valdez spill in Alaska's Prince William Sound, ExxonMobil has shelled out no more than ten cents on the dollar of the claims and awards levied against it. Meanwhile, Alaska's Prince William Sound and the people who depend on it endure continuing environmental, personal health, and economic damage.

The $20-billion fund set a preliminary target for damage claims that is tens of billions of dollars less than actual damages will be. It gave BP—a company that makes as much as $25 billion in profit in just one year—a four-year installment plan for paying out any money to settle claims. And it handed them a political, legal, and financial win, with the government and Kenneth Feinberg, the man appointed to oversee the fund, urging people not to sue. The public rationale for this recommendation was that it will speed money to the victims. But getting a quick dime to settle damages of a dollar or more doesn't make sense for anyone but BP—and for government agencies and officials that want to declare a victory and put the problem behind them.

There were other problems with the fund as well. One example: The claims deal allowed BP to secure the fund using future production from its leases in the Gulf of Mexico as collateral, and exempted all of BP's holdings elsewhere in the world. This locked the federal government into a partnership with BP, forcing it to continue to allow its offshore drilling in the Gulf to pay back the claims.

Just before Christmas 2010, Ken Feinberg—the lawyer who became a national figure by overseeing the fund for victims of the 9/11 terror attacks—confirmed some of my worst fears about the Gulf Coast Claims Fund. He made a blatant attempt to boost the number of cases the fund could say were "settled" (quotation marks because it definitely did not mean paid in full). He offered the spill's desperate victims one-time bonus payments of $5,000 for individuals and $25,000 for businesses, if they agreed to his settlement offers. The legal provisions were favorable in other ways to BP. To some, this was a reminder that it was ultimately BP that was paying Feinberg's substantial bill for his legal work. But in the bigger picture, it was also a revelation of how the government wanted to make the ordeal of contesting a big oil company go away without the involvement of pesky trial lawyers who had helped put Obama in office.

I had other plans. During the months we were fighting for the rights of the Gulf fishermen and for workers' ability to wear the proper safety gear, my law firm, bolstered by our high-visibility on environmental matters, was also assembling a long roster of clients who, like me, didn't want any part of the claims process that the Obama administration and BP had agreed to. In many ways, what was about to happen was the culmination of everything that I'd learned in my long war against Big Oil. When everyone else looked content to roll over and play dead, we fought to show the real effects of the Deepwater Horizon spill—that it was causing much greater harm to the Gulf Coast and its residents than either BP or the federal government was willing to admit, and that some of the things they were doing in the name of resolving the crisis were making people and wildlife even sicker.

We did this in part because it was Good Lawyering 101, because to get the most money for our clients we would need to build as damning a case against BP as humanly possible. But frankly, it was also good citizenship when we tried to get the right gear into the hands of the fishermen, or in the coming months when we warned people that Gulf seafood was not yet safe to eat. The government wasn't fighting for the people. Somebody needed to do it. I was ready.

On July 15, 2010, after oil had gushed into the Gulf for eighty-six days, uninterrupted, BP announced that a cap had finally stopped the spill. It would later be estimated that nearly five million barrels of oil had flowed into the Gulf. With the end of the active leak and with the $20 billion settlement fund in place, the news media stopped paying attention to the Gulf, and so did much of the nation.

But not us. Our battle with BP was just beginning.

PIRATES OF THE
GULF OF MEXICO

ON JUNE 14, 2010, President Barack Obama came down to the Florida Panhandle and ordered lunch. He said he had the seafood. I guess I'd have to just take his word for that. I wasn't invited. Neither was the news media.

Afterward, Obama did go before the cameras in Theodore, Alabama. Governor Bob Riley and a Greek chorus of Gulf cleanup workers were lined up behind him. The president decreed that on this day—fifty-four days into the crisis of the BP oil spill—he was launching "a comprehensive, coordinated and multiagency initiative" to make sure that the catch from the Gulf waters was safe to eat.

"Now, I had some of that seafood for lunch, and it was delicious," Obama said into the bank of cameras. "But we want to make

sure that the food industry down here as much as possible is getting the protection and the certification that they need to continue
their businesses." He concluded: "So let me be clear. Seafood from
the Gulf today is safe to eat. But we need to make sure that it stays
that way."

Away from the cameras, the environmental crisis in the Gulf continued to spiral out of control as the spring of 2010 was winding to
an end. The long plumes of foul-smelling crude were now coming
ashore as far away as the eastern Florida Panhandle, several hundred
miles from the collapsed rig. Indeed, the toxic goo was now coming
ashore on the pristine white-sand beaches near Pensacola, where the
local *Sun News* reported that "[t]he beach looked as if it had been
paved with a 6-foot-wide ribbon of asphalt, much different from the
tar balls that washed up two weeks earlier." Nearby, a family visiting
the Gulf Islands National Seashore found a young dolphin covered
in oil washed up on those sands.

The upbeat message from Obama in the midst of this was about
as clear as the muck fouling the beaches near Pensacola. In essence,
he was telling Americans to eat first, and ask questions later. How
could the president assure the public that seafood was safe to eat
when, as he acknowledged, in-depth testing hadn't even been carried
out yet? What's more, what most people didn't know is that the key
governmental agencies involved in the Gulf Coast recovery seemed
to be working harder to prevent independent scientists from doing
their own testing than they were at conducting their own rigorous
studies. I know this firsthand, since the team of experts I'd hired
were stymied at every opportunity they made to acquire independent
information.

The government seemed to have two agendas when it came to
seafood—both of them bad. One was siding with large commercial
fishing operations in the Gulf, whose livelihood depended on public
confidence in the safety of their catch, and not with the broader U.S.

public of seafood consumers. The other agenda was an effort to get the PR nightmare of the Deepwater Horizon aftermath, which was starting to erode confidence in both the White House and the behemoth of Big Oil, out of the headlines as quickly as possible.

In the months that followed, the federal government doubled down on its gamble that it could convince the public that there were no health risks associated with eating shrimp, grouper, oysters, and other seafood from the Gulf despite the presence of a couple of hundred million gallons of hydrocarbons in the water from which the seafood was obtained. The Pentagon even stepped in, placing a massive order for items that included a wide variety of shrimp, crab cakes, and even pre-packaged jambalaya that was sold at base commissaries around the world. At the White House, the executive chef bought more than 2,000 pounds of shrimp and other Gulf goodies from a supplier in the blue-collar sportsman's paradise of Venice, Louisiana, which he served at an array of holiday parties for Barack and Michelle Obama and their elite guests. The chef echoed the words of his powerful boss, that "we at the White House are so happy to play our part in reminding Americans that Gulf seafood is not only safe, but delicious."

The seafood shilling was just the beginning. There were declarations based on the highly flawed smell test protocol by the Food and Drug Administration that backed up the president's sweeping generalizations that the Gulf harvest met all safety standards. Meanwhile, the EPA was busy downplaying the toxic effect of the nearly two million gallons of a dispersant called Corexit that BP, against the advice of some government scientists, let loose in the Gulf to disperse the oil. It made the Gulf look cleaner, but the waters were actually more poisonous. Indeed, the National Oceanic and Atmospheric Administration (NOAA), another federal agency, issued rosy reports stating what BP wanted the public to hear, that the majority of the spill had simply disappeared.

The FAA implemented a temporary flight restriction almost immediately after the spill that continued for months across the entire eastern Gulf of Mexico. They refused to let the media get anywhere close to the offshore slicks. They even turned down Lisa Myers with NBC Nightly News, with whom I flew over the other stretches of the Gulf. The Coast Guard, for its part, turned the entire zone over to private security goons hired by BP who would not let anyone near the spill to photograph and take samples. Never before had America ceded its sovereign police powers to a corporation, and a foreign one at that. From the summer of 2010 on, the Obama administration and BP were on the same page—downplaying any lingering aftereffects. Their motives may have been slightly different—BP was still eager to limit its liability, while the feds wanted to help save BP by boosting the Gulf economy and to avoid political embarrassment—but the result was one and the same. The only real battle for justice for the American Gulf Coast was not going to come in the political arena, but would be fought through the civil courts.

Same as it ever was since I started taking on Big Oil more than two decades ago.

Even after the wellhead was finally capped that July, the number of people who came to me and my law firm—people devastated by the fallout from the spill and frustrated by their prospects of getting relief through the $20 billion BP compensation fund—grew exponentially. The bulk of them were the salt of the Louisiana earth, commercial and sports fishermen who've been pummeled not only by the public's understandable lack of confidence in Gulf seafood but also by the fact that many of the healthy fish that they used to catch in abundant numbers have simply disappeared.

"'CLOBBERED' BY THE OIL"

Near the height of the spill, I got a call from a well-known local charter boat captain named Al Walker, or "Captain Al," as he markets himself. It's a shame that, instead of grabbing a bite in Theodore, Alabama, President Obama didn't stop by Captain Al's Seafood, the simple restaurant that Walker was leasing out on the Mississippi Gulf Coast. He'd find lots of empty tables—pretty much the way it's been since the oil started spewing forth in April 2010.

There was agitation in Al Walker's voice as he told me his whole story. He was angry, bitter, and confused by the crossfire hurricane of events in the Gulf.

Now forty-three years old, Walker is a square-jawed, plain-talking creature of the Louisiana Bayou. Hailing from the low-lying fisherman town of Venice, Louisiana, near the wide mouth of the Mississippi— "the end of the earth," the locals call it—Walker had known a world where the only two ways to make a living were to head offshore, either on a fishing boat or the grueling but well-paying work aboard an offshore oil rig. "Captain Al" developed a passion for spearfishing, and some of the best spearfishing in the world takes place around the plethora of nearly 4,000 large rigs strewn around the Gulf waters off Louisiana. When he wasn't nailing large cobia and amberjack with his spear gun, Walker was capturing them on camera as one of the region's best underwater videographers. The beauty of the marine life that lurked in the metallic shadows of the rigs had made the sportsman Walker into an evangelist for Big Oil. For all his life, companies like BP not only kept the Gulf Coast humming but—unintentionally—their stark offshore structures had even made the sportfishing better. Then, in an explosive rush of fire, metal, and death, Big Oil had destroyed not just the Gulf but also Al Walker's perspective on the world.

"It's all about oil and seafood," he said, referring to the two totem poles of the Gulf economy, "and it's so ironic now that it's the oil killing the seafood." Walker told this to a television interviewer in June 2010, right around the time of Obama's seafood lunch and right before he contacted me about joining our lawsuit against BP and its rig contractors. That summer, he was still trying to make sense of the oily devastation he'd seen on his undersea dives. "We are losing our culture—our whole entire culture," he said, his voice tinged with plaintive desperation. "With no jobs and no seafood, this place is going to turn into Detroit overnight."

Hurricane Katrina, which flattened most of Venice, Louisiana, with its storm surge, had already forced Walker to pull up his stakes and move his charter boat business to the Mississippi coast, but he was still a booster for Big Oil. When he first heard of the disaster at the Deepwater Horizon spill, his initial reaction was the same as most of the other charter boat captains and commercial fishermen of the Gulf: He wanted to help.

Ironically, on the very day of the spill, Walker along with his wife and three-year-old son had moved back to the New Orleans suburb of Metairie, which he thought would be a big step in putting his life together after Hurricane Katrina. Instead, he was forced to cancel all his fishing charters, and he mostly just sat around his new home. Finally, on May 27, 2010, or thirty-six days after the *Deepwater Horizon* rig exploded, a BP contractor asked Al if he'd like to join the cleanup crew with his boat. He jumped at the opportunity, until he learned that there was nothing for him to do.

"I worked eight days—but it was all just a big show," he said, his voice still tinged with bitterness months later. "It was all for the cameras and the media. Nobody was doing anything that made a difference out there. All we did was drive down to the end of the river and sit there. I took the Coast Guard on a boat and all they did was sit on that boat all day; it was just a show to make the public think we were doing something." Meanwhile, it took days for Walker to figure out who was supposed to be paying him for this make-work, making it nearly impossible for him to actually collect the money he was owed.

Frustrated in his efforts to work for BP and unable to resume his charter boat business as the massive plume of oil expanded, Walker took on the only other work he could find: taking television news crews out to the edge of the spill and shooting footage with his underwater camera. He dove and recorded video for reporters from the local Fox affiliate in New Orleans, and then later for Discovery Canada, and other documentary crews. What he saw made him at least start to realize that BP hadn't been right about the extent of the environmental damage.

"When I went out there to film, I was on BP's side," he said of that first dive with the Fox team. "I thought it was a bunch of hype. I was going to prove to everybody that it's really not that big a deal. As a matter of fact, we didn't see any oil on the surface, but when I got down underwater—about 100 feet—it just clobbered me." After another dive later in the summer, Al reported on video: "It was the biggest kill I've seen yet. I will go out on a limb and say that billions of sea cucumbers are floating out there dead."

But in spite of what Walker saw underwater and his growing distress, he was still willing to work for BP and its cleanup contractors. When he learned that BP was looking for an experienced diver and underwater photographer to direct what was supposed to be a mission to locate and rescue oiled sea turtles, he jumped at the chance. He probably should have learned his lesson the first go-round.

"They strung me along for six months without letting me rescue one turtle—without sending me out there one day," he now recalls in amazement. He says there were frequent calls with BP officials and doctors about searching for the injured turtles, but nothing concrete was ever done. Ultimately, he said that BP did send some boats out looking for turtles, but not only was it not enough—just five boats over an expanse of 50,000 square miles—but also the crews that did go lacked experience and know-how. Walker says he believes that BP not only didn't want the horrible publicity of pictures of oiled turtles, but also officials were probably worried about the potential fines of $50,000 per turtle for producing evidence that its oil had harmed or even killed federally protected endangered species. To make matters worse, the *Los Angeles Times* and other news outlets reported that untold numbers of these rare turtles were getting killed in massive "burn boxes" where huge oil slicks packed with marine life were set on fire to limit the spill.

Increasingly, Walker was instead working with and spending time with folks who were allied with me as environmental activists— groups like the Sea Shepherds Society in the Gulf—and he began to consider retaining me as a lawyer. "There were a lot of good people out there trying to tell the truth, and they were all gravitating toward Stuart," he would say in an interview much later. "They really wanted the truth so they could make it public. That was the same way I felt."

By the time Al called my office, he had another, more personal reason to pick up the phone. His repeated dives into the oily waters had made him sick. Since the day that he'd shot the oil plume for the Fox TV crew, his hands had been covered in a bright red rash and his arms were pockmarked and scarred. There was blood in his urine and stool. One day, he even brought his buoyancy compensator and his regulator up the elevator to my law office on Canal Street. They were still all gunked up from the oil he discovered on that dive, fifteen months earlier.

The damage that Captain Al suffered from the BP spill is greater than anything he would have received from the $20 billion Gulf recovery fund, which is why he joined my growing lawsuit against the oil company and its contractors. But after Al Walker told me his story, I knew that he would also be an invaluable resource for us in pursuing our case against BP.

A BAND OF TRUTH-TELLERS

You see, I'd learned way back in the Street case that you can fight the power and the abuse of big corporations like BP with the courage of everyday citizens—decent folks who are smart and willing to work long hours and dig deep to gather the evidence we need to make a case. The template was created by the Street brothers up in Laurel, who in the process of righting the wrongs of Shell and Chevron became two of the best environmental case investigators in the business. But the Deepwater Horizon team was different. This wasn't a two-acre machine shop that had been ruined by Big Oil but a big swath of the 615,000-square-mile Gulf of Mexico.

We came together in the early days of the spill. On one side was the massive might of BP, a corporation with nearly $28 billion in revenues in the year before the Deepwater Horizon explosion, and its enablers in the federal government, who also had a near-stranglehold on the information that got released to the news media and thus to the public. On our side was a tiny band of scientists who weren't getting paid off by the government, a cadre of environmental activists, boat captains, and even an airplane pilot, all of whom refused to be told where they could or couldn't go.

You've heard of the "Pirates of the Caribbean," right? Our ad hoc band of environmental rebels could well have been called the "Pirates of the Gulf of Mexico." Not satisfied with the sanitized and sometimes flat-out incorrect version of the spill and its impact put out for public consumption, they took to the waters of the Gulf to take samples of seafood and water quality in areas where the government and BP clearly didn't want them snooping around.

Our team of truth-tellers included citizens like the previously mentioned Marylee Orr, the loquacious head of the Louisiana Environmental Action Network. With a big smile framed by her dark curly hair and her trademark blindingly bright tops, Marylee—an eclectic former art gallery owner who was moved to activism by her son's respiratory illness—brings the passion that only a native could have for saving Louisiana's remarkable yet endangered bayou. Marylee's unlikely chief ally was Wilma Subra—white-haired and bespectacled, looking every bit the grandmother from a Norman Rockwell painting—a chemist from Morgan City, Louisiana, and a woman who once won a MacArthur Foundation Genius Grant for her work in poor, heavily polluted communities. She and Marylee were a great team.

In the aftermath of the spill, I also worked closely with an iconoclastic, pony-tailed civil engineer named Marco Kaltofen, who teaches at Worcester Polytechnic Institute and runs his own testing firm. Dogged and matter-of-fact, Marco kept his freezer back home in Massachusetts absurdly stocked with a variety of dead crabs, shrimp, and other small aquatic animals that he'd plucked from the Gulf in the months after the spill and that he plans to save for research in years to come. But Marco is just one of a small group of academic scientists determined to study the effects of the BP spill without government interference. I also hired Dr. William Sawyer, a leading toxicologist, who intercepted untested seafood on the way from the Gulf to the marketplace.

In the end, we had almost created the equivalent of a "shadow agency" that was investigating the environmental impact of the BP spill at the same time as the federal government, but we were reaching wildly different conclusions. I hooked them up with Captain Al, who piloted them out to the critical danger zones. In the summer of 2011, when we started getting alarming reports of new oil bubbling up in the Gulf, we called again on a remarkable pilot—a longtime NASA physicist named Bonny Schumaker—who flies animal rescue missions when she's not photographing environmental disasters.

Yet in one important way, I saw how times had changed since the early days of the Street case, and that was the rise of the Internet.

No longer was the traditional media, which relied so heavily on government sources for its information, the only way to reach a large audience. Although I successfully provided key information about the situation in the Gulf to well-known mainstream reporters like Lisa Myers of NBC News and Ian Urbina of the *New York Times*, even appearing on CNN with Anderson Cooper, I also looked for new ways to spread the word about what we were finding. I launched my own blog, first called oilspillaction.com and now stuarthsmith.com, and within a short period of time I was getting 60,000 unique visitors a month from people seeking information about seafood safety and Gulf recovery. As the crisis unfolded, I also learned how to use the new social media tools of Facebook and Twitter to reach a wide audience.

And with the help of our remarkable team, we had quite a story to tell. These are the highlights:

SEAFOOD SAFETY

The government boasted in late 2010 that it had tested more than 10,000 seafood samples from the Gulf and found no evidence of problems, but the vast majority of those tests were what the National Oceanic and Atmospheric Administration called "sensory testing." You and I might call it a smell test, and that's hardly adequate for finding traces of hydrocarbons that are odorless, yet highly toxic. Meanwhile, Paul Orr, who is Marylee's son and also the unofficial river keeper for the lower Mississippi, gathered samples of shrimp, crab, and finfish from twenty different locations in the Gulf off the Louisiana and Mississippi coastlines and conducted tests that instead showed high levels of total petroleum hydrocarbons, even in seafood from areas that had been declared safe for fishing.

Testing by additional independent environmentalists from other areas of the Gulf showed high levels of cadmium, a long-lasting carcinogen, while other news accounts quoted Gulf fishermen who were reeling in red snapper with sores and lesions—some the size of a fifty-cent piece—the likes of which they had never seen before. The sick snappers shouldn't have been surprising, since the fish are bottom feeders—eating the shrimp and crabs who live on the sea floor—and independent scientists like Samantha Joye had already shown that oil from the leaking BP rig was coating the bottom of the Gulf. At the same time, crab fishermen were reporting their haul had dropped by 70 percent and the few crabs they did pull up suffered similar lesions and disease.

These problems persisted for several years. Oyster harvests east of the mouth of the Mississippi River remain precipitously low, and scientists who've studied how past oil spills have affected the reproductive health of marine life say that some of the worst impacts may be yet to come. Meanwhile, newer research has vindicated our earliest warnings about the government's seafood sampling. In August 2013, a report by Paul Sammarco of the Louisiana Universities Marine Consortium, which relied in part on the samples that we'd collected and saved in 2010, found that officials were likely far too hasty to re-open fishing areas in the Gulf. Sammarco found numerous problems with the way that NOAA had collected and tested its water samples—for example, not taking into account the patchy nature of the oil after so much dispersant had been sprayed.

Despite glowing reports from BP and the government that cleanup efforts were successful and that beaches were safe for swimming (again, dramatized by President Obama, who allowed a photograph of him swimming with his daughter Malia—in an unimpacted bay, of course—along the Florida Panhandle coast), oil continued to gunk up significant sections of coastline for years after the rig blew up.

In May 2011, river keeper Paul Orr visited and sampled spots on the Breton Island National Seashore—an environmentally critical bird sanctuary established in 1904 by President Theodore Roosevelt. He was alarmed by the smell of tar and the toxic, oily goo that he found. Paul reported "long trails of heavily oiled sand and scattered tar balls . . . spread along the center of the island" as well as lab results showing high concentrations of polynuclear aromatic hydrocarbons, the most toxic component of the BP oil spill. He took the samples after my pilot friend Bonny Schumaker spotted alarming signs of the pollution from the air.

The passage of time did not diminish the assault on the beaches; Tropical Storm Lee washed tar balls and patches of asphalt-like gunk along beaches up and down the Gulf in 2011, as did Hurricane Isaac in the summer of 2012. In 2013, more than three years after the Deepwater Horizon catastrophe, a blob of oil from the Macondo field that was roughly half the size of a football field came ashore in Grand Terre Island off the coast of Louisiana, and officials ordered a halt to fishing in the immediate area. LEAN was able to grab a sample from the tar mat and get it to Marco Kaltofen, who tested it and was shocked to find that it contained 100 percent undiluted petroleum product and was chock-full of carcinogens. "The tar mat sample contained the highest level of toxic and persistent polynuclear aromatic hydrocarbons (PAHs) that the team has ever found in Louisiana waters since the BP spill began in April 2010," he wrote. "The PAH level was three times higher than any other sample tested from Louisiana to Florida throughout the life of this oil spill."

Despite BP's efforts to rebut the real story of the devastation that was unleashed on marine creatures such as sea turtles and dolphins, my allies again uncovered evidence that the situation was heart-wrenchingly worse than the public knew. Consider the sea turtles: Some 600 of these magnificent creatures washed ashore dead or "stranded"—that typically means alive, but in a weakened condition—in 2010, which is six times the yearly average and is all but certainly because of the oil contamination from the *Deepwater*

Horizon. Incredibly, the numbers of dead and stranded turtles—many of them Kemp's ridleys, an endangered species—were running at nearly double that rate in the early months of 2011. The most outrageous part is that the spin maestros at BP and their defenders at NOAA insisted that the cause wasn't the 200 million gallons of oil or the large amount of toxic dispersant. They claimed shrimpers weren't deploying the right equipment to protect the turtles. Never mind that a lot fewer shrimpers were leaving the docks in the aftermath of the spill, or that most of 2011's stranded turtles came before the shrimping season even started. Once again, BP did all it could to limit its liability, since the fine for killing a Kemp's ridley is $50,000. Drawing attention away from the oil spill is one thing—dragging down the reputation of an entire industry and workforce in the process is a whole different kind of low (even by D.C. standards).

Then we had the fate of the poor dolphins. Between February 2010 and April 2011, 406 dolphins—many of them babies—were found either stranded or dead offshore. That was ten times the normal amount—serious enough that NOAA had little choice but to declare the deaths an "unusual marine event," or a UME. Again, this epidemic did not let up with the passage of time. In April 2013, the National Wildlife Federation reported infant dolphins were found dead at six times the average rates in January and February of that year and that more than 1,700 sea turtles—nearly seven times the average—were found stranded between May 2010 and November 2012, the last date for which information is available. Indeed, my own research team decided to take a look at sea nettles—a common food for dolphins in the Gulf—and, using the same testing protocols relied on by the EPA and other federal agencies, discovered alarmingly high levels of toxicity. Yet the bias on the part of the federal agencies tasked with protecting sensitive wildlife has been to look the other way.

There are a couple of reasons why oil—and oil-related contamination of seafood—has been so persistent in the Gulf. One reason is that in the early days of the spill, BP—despite some meekly-voiced trepidation from the Coast Guard and other federal officials—unleashed massive amounts of a chemical called Corexit to disperse the thick black oily plumes that had been visible for miles across the Gulf. The nearly two million gallons of the toxic Corexit that BP was permitted by the government to dump onto the spill in the spring and summer of 2010 achieved BP's goals. It got rid of the oil slicks that were becoming such a public relations disaster on the nightly TV news, and it stopped the oil from hitting the beaches and causing more economic devastation in the Panhandle tourism zones. Fish can't sue.

The problems that have been caused by the overuse and abuse of Corexit are particularly heartbreaking for me and for my team, because we had tried so hard, and so early in the oil-spill cleanup, to stop this from happening. On May 11, 2010, just three weeks after the rig explosion, I issued a statement criticizing the massive use of the toxic dispersant as having "the potential to cause just as much, if not more, harm to the environment and the humans coming into contact with it than the oil possibly would if left untreated."

Dr. William Sawyer and other toxicologists had told me that the active ingredient in Corexit, kerosene, would prove highly toxic both to marine life and to any humans who came in contact with it. "When you fly over the Macondo site where the *Deepwater Horizon* rig was located, the water looks like a gelatinous toxic soup thanks to this mix of dispersants and oil," he said after an aerial inspection that July. The enormity of what was happening was almost too much for folks to comprehend. In order to make the visible oil slicks on the surface—which were BP's worst public relations nightmare—disappear, they had essentially corroded large chunks of the Gulf, whether they knew it or not. The willy-nilly but government-approved use of the dispersants had also created even greater risks for the cleanup workers—risks that they had not been trained to deal with.

Laboratory tests performed for me by Worcester Polytechnic's Marco Kaltofen confirmed in our minds what many experts had feared about the Corexit spraying from day one, which was that dispersing the oil actually meant taking the toxic elements of the oil from the surface, where they were highly concentrated but weren't harming marine life below, and spreading them deep into the Gulf waters. Marco's tests back at his lab in Massachusetts were showing toxic pollution of water at levels thirty-five times higher than before the oil was dispersed.

Although the crisis of sick and dying dolphins and sea turtles received some attention in the media, journalists paid scant attention to reports of humans falling ill. There grew mounting evidence that oil-spill cleanup workers and other Gulf residents were suffering respiratory illnesses, skin rashes, and other more serious maladies because of their exposure to toxic air and tainted waterways. The federal authorities, of course, went to great lengths to insist that the sudden rise in such ailments was merely a coincidence. Donald Boesch, a member of Obama's Oil Spill Commission, summed up their response: "We were charged with being evidence-driven, and the fact is we've asked for and sought out evidence that the oil spill is the proximate cause of these health problems, and we just haven't found it."

But all Boesch had to do was walk into any of the doctors' crowded waiting rooms and health clinics scattered across the Gulf region. Or watch as Ray Mabus, the secretary of the Navy tasked with overseeing the reconstruction effort, heard from furious residents of Plaquemines Parish, Louisiana, about their health problems in August 2010. One of them, a fisherman named Acy Cooper, brandished a plastic bottle full of oily water from his local marsh at the secretary, pleading: "We ain't through the cleanup," he said. "We can't go into recovery. It is not recovery. Somebody's lying."

Around this time, Marylee reached out to a physician on the Gulf Coast, Dr. Michael Robichaux, of Mathews, Louisiana, to ask if he would examine some of the ailing cleanup workers. At first, Marylee later confided, the doctor was dubious that the ailments were linked to their exposure to BP's oil and the toxic dispersant. But after he began treating the fishermen and other coastal residents, he converted and became an evangelist for their cause. Nearly three years after the spill, Robichaux offered a moving report about the ongoing medical woes in a plea to a federal judge, stating that BP's proposed legal settlements needed to do much, much more for those who had been sickened.

"It appears that the interests of a large, foreign corporation have superseded the needs of thousands of Americans who reside along the coast of the Gulf of Mexico," Dr. Robichaux told U.S. District Judge Carl Barbier. "Equally as important to me, as a physician, is the fact that this settlement will result in a permanent record that completely ignores the truly significant illnesses that have resulted from this tragic event." Dr. Robichaux wrote that he's treated 113 patients who were exposed to toxic pollution from the BP oil spill, and about 100 of them have had severe chronic health effects, to the point that many of them are unable to work because of constant headaches or fatigue, relying instead on Social Security, Medicaid, or other social programs. Of the 113 patients that he's treated, Dr. Robichaux said that the most common symptoms are headaches (93), memory loss (89), fatigue (85), irritability (63), vertigo (60), nausea (49), and blurred vision (43), with others suffering from insomnia, persistent cough, or rashes. Of the twenty who experienced some sort of stomach pain, many reported it was severe. The exposure of these courageous first responders in the Gulf to a toxic cloud in the air is not much different from the pain and suffering of rescue workers at the World Trade Center after 9/11—except that the Gulf workers didn't have Jon Stewart crusading on their behalf.

This is why the fight for crude justice in the BP oil fiasco has been such an uphill battle. Indeed, you might be shocked at the lengths to which some government officials have gone to try to keep the true impact of the spill buried, metaphorically, and in some cases literally, 5,000 feet beneath the surface.

BEHIND BP'S ENEMY LINES

We realized what we were up against over the summer of 2010, roughly the same time that President Obama had declared to the nation that Gulf seafood was safe. I had already hired Sawyer—a top Florida-based research toxicologist with thirty years of experience—and civil engineer Marco Kaltofen to conduct the independent testing we would need to prove the toxic exposure and the damage done to my growing roster of clients. I brought them in because the fastest way to lose an environmental law case is to rely on industry or government data, as they rarely attempt to paint the full picture of what's going on. If you're doing environmental law, it's critical that you perform your own testing with your own experts—if you don't, you will lose every time. Throughout my career, I've never had an environmental case where the government was on the side of the victim.

I first learned about Marco's work when he came down to New Orleans to gather data from a major oil spill that took place at the Murphy Oil USA refinery after Hurricane Katrina. I knew that fingerprinting the oil in the Gulf and connecting it to the Macondo spill would be very important to any future litigation, and Marco was one of the top engineers in the field. (Marco describes himself by saying: "I specialize in when things go really bad.") The problem would be the lid of secrecy that BP and the feds had clamped down on the spill zone. On land, many of the roads leading to oil-gunked beaches had been blocked off by BP's private security guards. Out on the waters of the Gulf, however, it was a little more difficult for the authorities to restrict our movement.

Marco once flattered me by comparing what I do as an environmental trial lawyer to "a fourth branch of government." He's passionate about collecting evidence, and he's remarkably determined. "If someone doesn't get out there and collect physical evidence right from the get-go," he said, "it's all going to be the word of the oil companies. If you don't record the evidence of whatever happened...it's as if it didn't happen."

In the Deepwater Horizon case, Marco and Sawyer decided the best approach for taking on the restricted access was simply to look and act like he belonged. "We made sure we looked the part," he told me later. "We dressed the way the BP guys dressed—we had the story, we had the business cards and lab notebook and all the equipment. And you just go out there and you mix it up. If people ask questions, you tell the absolute truth—that I'm here to take samples, and this is who I work for."

Did it work? Soon, the BP cleanup contractors were giving Marco and his coworker access to their refreshment tent, handing them plates of food and bottled water.

"I got a Louisiana oysterman's license," Marco would later reveal. "I would get out to these sites and they would say, 'I'm sorry—you can't be collecting specimens out here.' I'd say, 'I got a Louisiana scientific collection permit—it cost twenty-five dollars from the Louisiana Department of Fish and Wildlife, and I would get BP escorts when I produced this document. It looked really official—it said I could collect oysters around this area. It had dates, stamps...."

From that, Marco collected a treasure trove of shellfish and marine life, as well as water, sand, and spilled oil—so much so, that a year later other independent scientists were coming to him begging for the opportunity to test his specimens. Their initial data showed alarming levels of toxic hydrocarbons, first in the Gulf water column and then in seafood. Even before they had issued any formal report, they started posting some of their raw data on the Internet.

That's when, out of the blue, they started getting phone calls from staffers on the president's commission investigating the oil spill.

"There was a grave concern as to why we were finding contamination," Sawyer recalled a short time later, when a local TV reporter asked him about the calls. "There was sort of a loaded question, and then the questions were geared toward whether we had sampling permits."

That's right. Instead of expressing concern about the danger that might be posed to American consumers from eating oil-contaminated seafood, these federal investigators were questioning if we had permits to collect our samples. Another case of secrets being more important than safety.

In another call, the investigators asked Marco if he thought the federal seafood data was wrong. But the tone of the question was hardly collegial. "Then he impugned my reputation and said they were trying to determine if we were sampling illegally." That's when the federal authorities told Marco that they were simply responding to a complaint from a food distributor—someone who would have a highly vested interest in covering up damaging data. Not surprisingly, the Oil Spill Commission pulled a 180-degree turn when a TV news crew investigated the calls and when a New Orleans–area congressman called for a full-blown investigation.

After the phone calls were exposed, one staffer even tried to explain that the calls to Marco and his associate went out because they were impressed with their work. We knew better. We had seen this kind of behavior from the very first days of the spill, when BP and their contractors and even the Coast Guard worked overtime to prevent citizen access to the spill zone. Even with all my years of fighting Big Oil and shoddy or lazy government enforcement, I was shocked that the government had tried to interfere with our independent investigation.

Much later, we learned from news accounts of some of the intense pressure that was taking place behind the scenes. At the same time that we were pressing for a more open investigation of the environmental impact, there was in-fighting between other independent scientists, who were finding equally troubling data, and government officials who found creative new ways to cover the scientists' data up. The Reuters news agency learned that wildlife biologists who'd been hired by the National Marine Fisheries Service to document the "unusual marine event"—the dramatic rise in dolphin deaths— by collecting specimens and tissue samples were then told that they couldn't make their findings known. The reason? They were told that the information needed to be kept under wraps because it was part of a law enforcement probe into the BP spill—always a ready-made excuse for government officials to keep secrets under wraps.

Of course, even when critical government testing was carried out, those tests were often inadequate for the complicated task of keeping the American people safe from such an unprecedented environmental catastrophe. Even when seafood passed that infamous "smell test" and the scientists actually determined the levels of hydrocarbons and other toxins, the standards were still inadequate. According to the government testing structure, the "safe" consumption level for a grown man is four shrimp per week. Who the hell living on the Gulf of Mexico eats only four shrimp per week? Many of us, myself included, eat shrimp several times a month and I can tell you that I eat a lot more than four at a sitting, maybe something closer to fourteen. Down on the Gulf, four isn't a consumption level—hell, it ain't even a shrimp cocktail.

Marco insists that there are other major problems with the way that government scientists are checking for seafood safety. About those so-called smell tests, in which the specimens that were clearly oiled in the spill or possibly diseased were getting tossed aside? As Marco pointed out, that means that the results of actual lab testing—in-depth chemical analysis for polynuclear aromatic hydrocarbons (PAHs) and other toxins—were skewed, because the seafood that would have produced the worst numbers was getting tossed into trash buckets. "So it made the numbers look a lot better for everybody," Marco says. "They made it look a lot better by not testing fish!" In the summer of 2011, some fifteen months after the well explosion, Marco said he was still testing crabs contaminated with oil that bore the chemical fingerprint of the BP spill.

The real agenda in Washington seemed to be to shield the oil giant from legal liability, and shield the Obama administration from political blame. Few folks wanted to accept the reality of what the cleanup workers had seen and suffered out on the Gulf.

One of the charter boat captains who ended up coming to Marylee for help was Louis Bayhi. Like most of the Gulf fishing fleet workers, Louis is a colorful character—he was a bullfighter for a while before he took to the water, and today his Louisiana accent is as thick as an overcooked bowl of gumbo. But when he spoke at a rally of Gulf workers and environmental activists working with LEAN, his voice was drained of joy.

"The last six or seven months have been pretty devastating for me and my family," Louis told the LEAN rally. When he spoke, it was hard not to be reminded of how similar his tale was to the plight of the workers who raced into Ground Zero after 9/11 and became seriously ill as a result. "When the spill started," he said, "we wanted to get out and get it cleaned up as quickly as possible—do whatever it takes."

Louis said he was very trusting of BP and its contractors, at least at first. In training classes, they told him there'd be no need for protective gear because his boat would be hugging the coastline and not going anywhere near where the crude oil was gushing forth—even though when he took to the Gulf he brought workers as close to the site as three miles. When he and some of his colleagues came back to the BP tents at the end of the day feeling nauseous, they were told it was seasickness, even though Louis told the rally, to hoots and laughter, that the only time he'd ever been seasick was when he had beer for breakfast. When two workers on his boat were overcome by fumes one day and passed out, Louis knew this was in fact no laughing matter.

But by then it was too late.

For Louis, the economic devastation came first. He says that BP owed him, by his accounting, $225,000—money that of course was meant to replace all the charter boat business that was lost after the spill. Soon, he lost his house, and he, his wife, and their two young daughters were forced to move in with his relatives, and then the bank repossessed his vehicles. He said he had to borrow his grandfather's truck to come speak at the rally. His health came next.

"Five days I was in the hospital with abdominal pains and a tube down my stomach, and they couldn't tell me why," he said, his voice breaking. "They told me I had a kink in my bowel but they wasn't sure. They ran CAT scans and everything else.... I don't have health insurance anymore."

In hindsight, it's hard for Louis to believe how naive he was. He's still haunted by a couple of incidents. One is the time he took some marine biologists from Florida State University out to collect fish samples. Remarkably, he and his crewmate cooked up and ate some of the rest of the catch that day—only later did he learn that the tests that the scientists performed showed that "we ate fish with more toxins in them than are allowed anywhere in the world."

The extreme efforts of a Big Oil giant to avoid liability for their actions were sadly familiar. But the actions of the government to side with a huge multinational corporation and against the health and safety of American workers were unconscionable.

And it was clear to all of us who called the shots. For weeks after the spill, Marylee pressed for admission to the main command center; federal regulations state that non-governmental organizations like LEAN are supposed to have that access. When she finally was allowed inside to meet with officials from BP and from agencies like the Coast Guard and NOAA, she saw who was in charge: officials from BP. She reported back later: "Our government did not seem to have authority over what was going on."

Around the same time, Marylee and some other environmental activists from the Gulf got a private meeting with a top federal official—EPA administrator Lisa Jackson, who is a native of Louisiana. The main item on their agenda was to convince the feds to force BP to stop spraying large quantities of the dispersant Corexit in the Gulf, especially since we produced evidence supporting that Corexit was merely hiding the oil and spreading toxins over a larger area. (Others reached the same conclusion; Hugh Kaufman, longtime EPA employee and whistleblower, said government officials were well aware of the hazards of Corexit, telling an interviewer that "in the Exxon Valdez case, people who worked with dispersants, most of them are dead now. The average death age is around fifty. It's very dangerous, and it's an economic...protector of BP, not an environmental protector of the public.")

At first it seemed like Jackson was listening to Marylee's plea; a short time later, in late May, the EPA and the Coast Guard issued a joint order to BP telling the company to "eliminate" surface spraying of Corexit—unless the firm got a waiver from the Coast Guard because of exceptional circumstances.

You can guess how that all played out. BP asked for and routinely got a waiver from the Coast Guard to spray Corexit—day after day, including nine days in a row immediately after Lisa Jackson's "order" and ultimately seventy-four times over fifty-four days. We estimate as many as a million gallons of the toxic dispersant were deployed in the Gulf after the government's supposed command to eliminate much of its use.

"I was astonished," Marylee said later. "This was a corporation—not from the United States—that had caused the worst environmental devastation in American history."

I did find that my long history of dealing with Big Oil and their patterns of abuse proved to be extremely helpful in exposing their tricks. When it came to the oil giants and pollution, I knew where the bodies were buried, so to speak. Or more accurately, where the oil was buried. Remember towns like Brookhaven, Mississippi, where the waste from oil production was simply dumped in unlined pits? When it comes to waste products, the philosophy of Big Oil was "out of sight, out of mind." That's why I think BP was so eager to deploy massive amounts of Corexit, which didn't get rid of oil toxins but spread them out so that the ocean surface looked cleaner. That same mentality drove another insidious method that BP used extensively: land farming.

Land farming is still the same insidious practice that Richard Brackin encountered when he tried to enforce the radiation regulations in Louisiana: taking oily waste by-products and mixing them with soil, with the idea that microorganisms along with the soil itself will break down the oil and dilute it. Sometimes, fresh soil is brought in to cover up the contaminated dirt underneath. Like I said, out of sight, out of mind. By early July 2010, at the height of the cleanup, a film crew captured footage of workers blending oil with the once-pristine sands of Grand Isle, the environmentally delicate barrier island south of New Orleans. A large Hyundai backhoe sat atop the dunes, moving clean sand atop the dirty.

The solution to pollution is dilution—that's what the oil companies always say. Unfortunately, that's not really true, especially with land farming because it will basically contaminate the ecosystem in which it's buried for a long, long time. It will continuously leach into the environment and impact the surrounding vegetation and wildlife. It will kill the marshes and the marine life that lives there. Instead of the environment healing the toxic waste, the toxins continue to destroy the environment they're hidden in. Despite my blowing the whistle on the land-farming activities, state and federal regulators did nothing.

A month after I exposed BP's land-farming techniques, there were reports that the oil behemoth had rolled out a new piece of heavy machinery along the beaches of the Gulf Coast: a Sand Shark. The Mobile *Press-Register* observed one such Sand Shark as it worked the coastline near Baldwin, Alabama. "Bright orange and emblazoned with BP logos, the Sand Shark dismantled any doubt that there is a significant amount of oil sitting just below the surface of Baldwin's sandy vistas," the newspaper reported. "After tilling a stretch of less than fifty feet, the Sand Shark's hopper was filled with a mash of shell shards and emulsified oil."

It was clear, unfortunately, that the thick and foul-smelling residue would be leaving its nasty stain across some of the most vital beaches and marshes of the Gulf for a long time—even if not another drop had flowed once the well was reported capped in the summer of 2010. But it had also always been the fear of my environmental team that the event was not really over, that the damage caused by the explosion might cause oil to flow forth from new leaks, possibly from cracks in the sea floor near the capped wellhead.

But even as the catastrophe entered its second full year, public access to the site remained seriously restricted. For many months after the spill, the FAA maintained a no-fly zone over the spill site, allowing virtually no air traffic under a height of 3,000 feet, a distance above which it would be virtually impossible for citizens or members of the news media to shoot clear pictures or video of the oil. At the worst of the Deepwater Horizon crisis, the FAA's zone of temporary flight restriction, or TFR, stretched from the middle of Louisiana to the eastern panhandle of Florida, which is close to 500 miles. Typically, news organizations are granted a waiver to do their reporting, but in the case of the BP oil spill such requests were turned down.

Luckily, in the aftermath of the Deepwater Horizon tragedy I met a remarkable pilot named Bonny Schumaker. A longtime physicist for NASA, Bonny had a second life as a humanitarian flying ace, in the cockpit of her souped-up Cessna 180, nicknamed Bessie. She started out flying animal rescue missions, delivering scores of often neglected or even abused dogs and cats to new homes hundreds of miles away through an organization called On Wings of Care. Increasingly, Bonny was drawn to environmental causes, and she departed from her home in California to New Orleans not long after she learned about the BP spill. From May 2010 through the end of the year, she logged more than 300 hours over the Gulf, escorting news crews and the photographer that I had brought onto my team, Jerry Moran. Her commercial pilot's license and her NASA credentials provided access that other pilots didn't have, and she brought back the pictures that BP didn't want anyone to see—of tar-soaked beaches and oiled birds and miles of oil plumes beyond what BP and the feds were admitting to the general public.

Bonny came back to the Gulf a number of times in 2011. That summer, I learned from a longtime source that fresh oil was creating a new plume near the Macondo site. A second source—one with close ties to BP—confirmed the tip, and said that as many as forty boats were involved in a new containment effort. The reaction of the Coast Guard and BP to our report? They denied it, of course. That's when Bonny told me she wanted to check it out from the air.

On August 19, 2011, Bonny and her trusty Cessna, Bessie, took to the air over the Gulf for four hours with two photographers from the Gulf Restoration Network. They were appalled at what they found—oil, lots of it, with the heaviest concentrations in the immediate vicinity of the Deepwater Horizon site. One of the photographers, Jonathan Henderson, reported the findings to the U.S. Coast Guard and later wrote that the oil seemed to be clustered in round formations.

"I have no idea why or how this could happen and neither did the [Coast Guard] official," Henderson wrote. "The formations are clearly rainbow in color and in some cases have also a brownish tint."

The blog posts that I wrote about both the initial report from our sources and from Bonny's subsequent flyover caused a sensation and were re-posted on Web sites around the world. Still, it wasn't a shock when both BP and the Coast Guard continued to deny that any fresh oil was leaking from the Macondo site in the pages of New Orleans's daily newspaper, the *Times-Picayune*. But their fairy tales about the true conditions in the Gulf were getting harder to maintain. One commendable journalist, Ben Raines of the Mobile *Press-Register*, went beyond BP's denials and decided to investigate for himself. Five days after Bonny's mission, Raines reported discovering hundreds of oily patches within a mile of the Macondo wellhead, bearing a "pronounced and pungent petroleum smell." What's more, Raines turned over samples to two experts from LSU, who confirmed that the fingerprint of this new oil was a dead ringer for oil from BP's *Deepwater Horizon*.

You would think the experience would have humbled BP and the Coast Guard, but the August 2011 flap proved to be the first of several times in which Bonny discovered, and we reported, that fresh oil sheens—significant in size—were covering the Gulf in areas very close to where the *Deepwater Horizon* had exploded. In the late summer of 2012, we repeated the cycle—with BP and the Coast Guard initially seeking to deny or at least downplay Bonny's new reports, hoping to deflect the very legitimate worries that natural fissures caused by BP's botched well were continuing to taint the Gulf. In late November 2012, the Coast Guard ordered BP to send robotic submarines down to the floor of the Gulf and take other measures to locate the sources of the fresh oil. It was another victory—arguably a Pyrrhic victory in the war to restore the Gulf.

I can't say enough about the remarkable public service that Bonny Schumaker has performed, but like most of the public service that's been performed in the Gulf since April 21, 2010, her good deeds have not gone unpunished. Just like the boat captains Al Walker and Louis Bayhi, her trips to the site of the oil slick have resulted in sore throat and flu-like symptoms—this from a woman who never gets sick. After hundreds of hours over the BP spill, her hands are red, blistered, chafed, and peeling—just like Al Walker the first time he came into my office.

My greatest fear is that the symptoms we're seeing now among the Gulf workers and volunteers form the leading edge of a public-health disaster. I share that anxiety with many folks down here. At the LEAN rally, Louis Bayhi spoke of taking a break from his cleanup duty by taking his family to a nearby beach; his daughters went for a long dip in a section of the Gulf that was opened for swimming, just 100 yards from where heavy machinery was throwing oily sands in the air. He said blood tests of his daughters now show more toxic contamination than his own.

"The Good Lord will take care," Louis said through thick sobs. "I praise God every day and hope I can watch my little girls grow up." Those words send shivers down my spine, because they remind me so much of what the young people of Laurel, Mississippi, had said after building sand castles and making mud pies from the poisonous, radioactive silt that big oil companies had dumped on their land.

On the legal front, I never stopped doing battle for my clients. In early May 2012, BP announced that it had reached a settlement deal—estimated at the time to be worth $7.8 billion—with a circle of well-connected tort lawyers called the Plaintiffs Steering Committee on behalf of the Gulf Coast residents and small businesses like my clients. I joined a handful of other lawyers who went before Judge Barbier in September 2012 to object to the proposed deal. How could a price be fixed on the damage caused by BP when new oil keeps coming ashore, as happened when Hurricane Isaac hit the Gulf Coast just days before the courtroom arguments? Backed by Dr. Robichaux's testimony, we argued that the deal was woefully inadequate for those who had been made ill by exposure to the toxic soup of crude oil and Corexit, and also that its terms were unfair and arbitrary for so many coastal businesses that had been hammered in 2010 and beyond by the loss of tourism and other economic activity. We didn't win that skirmish, but the legal battles continue to this day—spurred on, remarkably, by BP executives who have the gall to say they're paying too much. I have pledged to fight to make BP pay every last dollar for all the pain that it's caused, until the last gavel comes down.

It is a long slog. By the fourth anniversary of the spill in 2014, my firm has successfully handled claims against BP for about three-quarters of our thousands of clients, but hundreds of them—restaurant owners or fishing boat captains who took a huge hit in 2010 and have struggled to bounce back—were still fighting for their fair share. There's no Big Bang in a case like this, no denouement to match that sweltering day when a jury foreman wrote down that "one billion dollars" verdict against ExxonMobil. But I came to realize that our arduous and sometimes quixotic crusade to get justice for the Gulf was worth it. I'll admit there were days, early on, when we felt like voices in the wilderness. But by the third anniversary of the catastrophe in the spring of 2013 something fairly incredible had happened. For one thing, the federal government, whom we'd been hectoring for its passive response, showed signs of at least partially growing a spine.

BP spent literally hundreds of millions of dollars to sway public opinion through a series of slick commercials that were hard to avoid when you turned on a TV. We had a few smart scientists and lawyers and a blog—and we were winning the PR showdown. Three years after the spill, the conventional wisdom had swung to our side—that things were not back to normal, that the spill had caused great and lasting damage to wildlife, seafood safety, and human health, and that unfortunately the problems in the Gulf would persist for years to come.

The BP experience changed me in one other way. Although I'd been fighting pitched battles against Big Oil since the end of the 1980s, the Deepwater Horizon debacle—and what it said about America's broader addiction to oil—caused me to take a step back, to think more about the big picture. The bad behavior that I'd witnessed in Mississippi, in Kentucky, and off the coast of Louisiana wasn't just a case of a few sleazy actors, but was endemic to the way that we fueled our nation. A lifetime of ferreting out the oil industry's secrets in a courtroom had convinced me that the fight against the folly of our fossil-fuel culture had to take place on a wide front, and it had to involve all of us.

With the arrival of even riskier practices like fracking for natural gas, and with increased knowledge about the role that fossil fuels were playing in causing climate change, it was time to talk about radical change, to go from advocate to activist.

NINE

BETTING ON
PLANET EARTH

T HEY USED TO CALL THE EIGHTY-MILE STRETCH of the Mississippi
River that runs from Baton Rouge all the way to New Orleans
"the petro-chemical corridor." This land of gentle river bends and
thick groves of bald cypress is now pockmarked and carved up with
glistening metal pipeline and rusty smokestacks. Louisiana is blessed
and cursed by its geography—rich marshes and swamplands sitting
atop the massive oil deposits of the Gulf region, as well as massive
salt domes, all at the mouth of the industrial waterway of North
America. But it was little more than a generation or two after Big
Energy, chemicals, and plastics took over Louisiana that this stretch
of land gained a new nickname.

Now they call it "Cancer Alley." In fact, research shows that Louisiana has the second highest cancer rate in the nation.

In Baton Rouge, at the northern cul-de-sac, if you will, at the end of Cancer Alley, sits the humble, working-class, predominantly black neighborhood of Standard Heights. The neighborhood grew up in the shadows of the nation's second-largest oil refinery, which was built by the old Standard Oil Co. (hence the name) but today is operated by ExxonMobil. Today, only a handful of local folks from this economically depressed community get jobs at the plant.

Just to the immediate north of Standard Heights, a whopping 500,000 barrels of oil are processed every day on the Eastbank of the Mississippi at this century-old site that also now includes a sizable chemical plant. Its sprawling tank farm and matchstick-like array of smokestacks, usually shrouded in white smoke, dominate the view from Interstate 110 and from atop the massive capitol skyscraper that Huey Long erected. It is only in recent years that folks in Standard Heights have come to see the ExxonMobil plant there for what it really is, a monster.

On the night of May 7, 2012, phones started buzzing with text messages and were ringing off the hook at the offices of the Louisiana Bucket Brigade, an environmental group that rose up to fight for public health and for a cleaner environment in Cancer Alley. Although residents of Lupine Avenue near the gates of the giant ExxonMobil facility were used to the smell of rotting eggs or the occasional headache or nausea that came with it, this was clearly an unusual event.

"…[T]his is Bessie Johnson…and I smelled something yesterday, more of a rotten egg type smell and I really didn't see anything," stated one call report. "And I'm currently smelling gas in my house and I had it checked and I have yet to get reported that I have a gas leak."

"There's a bad smell in the area and it has me feeling nauseous," said another.

"It's a bad smell in the neighborhood...extremely...can't hardly breathe," another said.

The Bucket Brigade received more than a dozen reports from the neighborhood that night, including one that compared the odor to "bad meat." But when the environmental activists contacted the Louisiana Department of Environmental Quality, the DEQ said it had already been in touch with ExxonMobil, which said there were no problems at the plant. That was pretty much what they always said.

A month later, it happened again. When Standard Heights residents were complaining of severe headaches from the new odors, ExxonMobil finally confessed that there had been a small problem in the chemical plant. The oil giant told the DEQ regulators that there had been an accidental release at the plant after a bleeder plug failed on a tank for at least several hours in the middle of the night; the tank contained something called "steam-cracked naphtha." But the real main ingredient was the cancer-causing chemical benzene. Because of its toxicity, the trigger for reporting an accidental release of benzene is just ten pounds, and ExxonMobil initially told the state that they were looking at "a ten-pound event."

Residents feared something much worse. One woman over in Standard Heights named Tonga Nolan later told NPR that her daughter was vomiting so badly they took her to an emergency room, while another resident said that he gathered up his family and drove them out into the country, to get away from the smell.

Although reportable, barely, the ten-pound trigger did not motivate an aggressive response from the DEQ to warn and possibly evacuate parts of Standard Heights near the plant. Meanwhile, plant workers contacted the Bucket Brigade to report that in fact hundreds of gallons of toxic chemicals had been simply dumped into the sewer system in the event. That complaint caused the DEQ to reconnect with ExxonMobil, which was now acknowledging that 1,300 pounds of benzene spewed forth, significantly higher than the originally reported ten pounds. The day after that, ExxonMobil told the state it had new information. The difference in the numbers was now staggering: 28,688 pounds of benzene, 10,882 pounds of toluene, 1,110 pounds of cyclohexane, 1,564 pounds of hexane, and 12,605 pounds of other volatile organic compounds (VOCs)—all wafting toward Standard Heights in the dead of night, while residents were sleeping in their beds, uninformed.

The incorrect information that was handed out by the world's largest oil company—underestimating the spill by a factor of 2,800 (if their final version can even be trusted!)—was just one indicator of much larger problems at ExxonMobil Baton Rouge, and dozens of chemical plants and refineries much like it across the United States. As NPR noted in an investigative report, state data that it analyzed showed that in the three years up through 2001 the ExxonMobil Baton Rouge facility put out nearly 4 million pounds of VOCs with approval from regulators.

And that was just a small fraction of the VOCs that were released from similar facilities in Texas, Louisiana, California, and elsewhere; scientists who've studied the issue say that energy and chemical companies typically (whether purposefully or not) underestimate the release of these airborne toxins—the same ones, you'll recall, that sickened so many cleanup workers in the Deepwater Horizon catastrophe—by a huge order of magnitude. And yet like so many other environmental boondoggles, government regulators seemed either unequipped or unwilling to deal with the problem.

Of course, it should have been easy for ExxonMobil to fix the problems itself. Remember, this was a company that made $44.9 billion in profits—let me repeat that, $44.9 billion!—in 2012, the year that the leak occurred. That was just a few million short of the all-time profit record for any corporation in the history of the planet. And much of its added income that year came from oil-refining operations such as the one in Baton Rouge. But around the 1990s, right as the corporation's cash flow was on the verge of increasing, ExxonMobil cut back on its routine maintenance, as well as its staffing, at its refineries.

Ironically, inspectors for the U.S. EPA, who tend to be a tad tougher than the regulatory toothless tigers of Louisiana, happened to be conducting an inspection of the Baton Rouge site in the summer of 2012. What the team discovered, according to NPR's investigation, is alarming—although sadly, not too surprising when you know the track record of Big Oil.

The EPA inspectors found "significant corrosion on a majority of the pipes" in a key area of the plant called the hydrocracker, critical areas of the plant where valves were wrapped in garbage bags secured with duct tape, extensive corrosion of pipes in the sections of the ExxonMobil facility where gasoline, diesel, and jet fuel are produced; overdue inspections on some pipes that turned out to be leaking or had already burst; and a string of serious accidents and leaks that had not been reported to regulators as required by law. You might think that these findings would have serious consequences for the world's most powerful oil company. But more than a year after the EPA inspection, the government had yet to take any action against ExxonMobil at all. In fact, the public only found out about conditions at the Baton Rouge facility because an activist named Anna Hrybyk from the Louisiana Bucket Brigade filed a Freedom of Information request that forced EPA to release the damning reports.

Finally, on June 14, 2013, the one-year anniversary of the large underreported leak, my law firm, SmithStag, joined with residents of Standard Heights to take action. We filed a class action suit against ExxonMobil in an East Baton Rouge court, seeking damages on behalf of residents as well as seeking to force the oil giant to make the much needed inspections and to upgrade the failing pipes that had spewed so much toxic air into a working-class neighborhood.

You should by now have a clear-eyed sense of the way that environmental justice works—and doesn't work—in the middle of the 2010s. Big Oil dumps toxic materials on a poor and politically unempowered neighborhood, and the supposed government watchdogs look the other way. Finally, it's the citizens, not their governmental representatives, who call attention to the problem. But at the end of the day there is only one venue where they even have a chance of redressing their grievances, the civil court.

THE INSANITY OF "EXTREME ENERGY"

On one hand, I have been forced throughout much of my career as an environmental tort lawyer to fight even to keep that door open—thanks to Big Oil's highly paid lobbyists and the legislators' lobby. In Mississippi, we've fought the rise of the state Oil and Gas Board, while in Louisiana there is an effort in the state legislature every year to bar what the oil companies had labeled "legacy lawsuits," which really means trying to stop owners of polluted land from winning justice in the courts. At the same time, as the political power and influence of energy companies continue to grow larger, I also still see the limits of civil actions as the only available means to check their unjust enrichment.

Think about it. In the mid-2000s, I virtually watched as ExxonMobil wrote a $200 million check—$200 million!—for its unconscionable behavior in Harvey, Louisiana, where it shipped highly radioactive scale for years, sickening workers like Milton Vercher and Lee Dell Craft while fully knowing the risks. Now, just seventy-five miles up the Mississippi River, at the same time it was paying a hefty tab for those damages, ExxonMobil was refusing to modernize or even inspect its rusty pipes at a giant, ancient refinery and chemical plant, spewing toxins into what—until now, anyway—had been an unsuspecting neighborhood. Wasn't that the whole point of tort law—to keep bad actors from acting badly? To make the cost of doing good less than the cost of doing bad? But the check that ExxonMobil wrote for trashing the Grefer property near the Westbank of the Mississippi, large as it was, clearly wasn't enough of a penalty to inspire ExxonMobil to become a better corporate citizen, not even in the state where it wrote the check. Maybe that's not surprising, since it only took a day and a half of charging you $3.50 a gallon at the pump for ExxonMobil to make all the money back.

There's an old saying among political activists that you're probably familiar with: Think globally, act locally. For me, the process had kind of happened in reverse. I'd started learning about the environmental sins of Big Oil in very local, very isolated ways, in places like Laurel, Mississippi, and Harvey, Louisiana, because I wanted a big case, and clients who needed a good lawyer. And when I did think about policy matters, like regulation of radioactive oil wastes, it wasn't part of a broader philosophy about U.S. energy practices. I was a kid who grew up in Louisiana in the 1970s, and so the ways of the oil patch—the recruitment ads for working on offshore rigs, the oil company skyscrapers that line Poydras Street in New Orleans— just seemed like the way that life was supposed to be in America.

But the BP case changed me, and it changed my worldview about fossil fuels. I started my blog up shortly after the spill in order to get real information out to the people who needed it; I initially focused on the immediate crisis in the Gulf. There was certainly a lot to write about there—but gradually I focused more and more on the bigger picture of Big Oil. There were a lot of interconnections. In 2011, I was interviewed for a remarkable documentary about the BP spill called *The Big Fix* by filmmakers John Tickell, a New Orleans native, and his wife Rebecca Harrell Tickell. The documentarians reached the same conclusion as my team of experts, that the abuse of the dispersant Corexit had wreaked environmental havoc on the Gulf, and that ongoing oil leaks at the site meant the crisis was far from over. When I saw the final cut, it helped convince me that the Deepwater Horizon was not an isolated incident, but intrinsically linked with a string of risky and careless practices by Big Oil around the globe. What had become clear was that BP's accident in the Gulf, exceptional as it was, was also all but inevitable. It was the consequence of a global shift in the way that we produce and consume energy.

The need for fuel to power cars, laptops, and refrigerators is greater than ever—especially as the huge developing economies of India and China rise to western levels of prosperity. But that fuel is harder to get; the era of "easy oil" that sits directly under the flat open expanses of the Texas prairie or the sands of the Saudi Arabian desert is winding down and will probably end sometime in our twenty-first century.

Many environmentalists hoped that growing talk about the world nearing or possibly at "peak oil"—a concept still hotly debated among the best scientists—would finally inspire the United States to join other nations, most notably those in Europe, in a push toward a new strategy that would embrace "green energy." That would surely put an end to the dominance of the oil giants, once customers had access to power that was renewable, and thus cleaner and cheaper. Indeed, running to become the forty-fourth president in 2008, nearly two years before the Deepwater Horizon disaster, President Obama declared that renewable energy would be a focus of his presidency. "We simply cannot pretend...that we can drill our way out of this problem. We need a much bolder and much bigger set of solutions. We have to make a serious, nationwide commitment to developing new sources of energy and we have to do it right away."

But that's not what happened. The scarcity of oil during the latter years of the 2000s caused oil prices to spike and after the dust of the 2008 economic crisis had settled, the price for a barrel of oil had landed at or near $100 a barrel. Coupled with a related spike in natural gas prices, Big Oil profits soared in tandem with risky types of exploration. By the first year of President Obama's second term, U.S. oil production was, surprisingly, at its highest level in twenty years, and imports of foreign crude had dropped substantially. In 2012 alone, American oil production spiked by one million barrels a day—the biggest jump of any nation in the world, and the fastest U.S. rise since 1967. Many voters were pleased, and understandably so, because the higher energy production at home seemed to be keeping prices stable, at least, at the gas pump and promised to reduce messy American entanglements in the Middle East.

Obama certainly used this as a selling point for his successful 2012 reelection, but the reality was that this was not at all what he'd promised for his first term. Solar and wind generation did increase slightly thanks to roughly $90 billion that the president placed in his 2009 economic stimulus package, but by 2011 they still accounted for just 3 percent of U.S. power generation; the comparable numbers in industrialized Germany are roughly four times as much, and growing much more quickly. Likewise, other Obama initiatives that would have reduced the burning of fossil fuels—electric battery-powered cars and high-speed rail, for example—have lost momentum, although in fairness much of the blame falls on ultra-conservative Republican lawmakers who opposed any form of government spending.

Indeed, oil companies are winning the political debate right now; their victory has been gained on the back of new technology that has allowed for new drilling in extreme environments where energy extraction was not feasible just a generation ago. By capturing the oil and natural gas under deep expanses of ocean, even in the icy waters of the Arctic, in once inaccessible formations like the Canadian tar sands, and in pockets of oil and natural gas trapped inside shale rock formations, Big Energy has found new ways to feed America's addiction to fossil fuels. The risks of this phenomenon are enormous—in the daily degradation of air pollution, the release of greenhouse gases and the copious production of radioactive wastes, and in the catastrophic risk of exploding rigs, pipeline ruptures, and runaway trains.

Michael Klare, a professor at Hampshire College, has written extensively about the rise of what he called "extreme energy," unconventional sources that are changing the way we produce and consume energy. He explained in a 2013 interview with Oilprice.com that "the production of oil and gas is not a static phenomenon but is undergoing profound changes, involving greater risk to the environment and greater risk of conflict over disputed sources of supply (such as offshore and Arctic reserves). These risks are bound to multiply as all sources of 'easy' oil disappear and we become increasingly reliant on hard-to-reach, hard-to-process 'extreme' energy. Only through the accelerated development of renewables can we avoid an inevitable spiral of war and disaster."

Klare believes that society is in denial about the threat to the environment and to human welfare that's posed by the hunt for extreme energy, and I agree. The facts behind Big Oil's resurgent production should disturb you.

OFFSHORE DRILLING

On December 31, 2012, a large offshore drilling rig called the Kulluk, which belongs to Royal Dutch Shell, was being towed to port in Seattle. Instead, it broke loose and was pushed by brutal winds—through the frigid Arctic waters off of Alaska, unmanned and out-of-control. The rig, which contained more than 150,000 gallons of diesel fuel and oil, finally crashed on the rocks near tiny Sitkalidak Island; in a stroke of remarkable good fortune, none of the oil spilled in environmentally sensitive waters that are home to harbor seals, salmon, sea lions, and several endangered species. Soon, investigators unraveled the real reason the rig was on the move at the most dangerous time of the year. Shell—a company that made just over $25 billion in worldwide profits in 2012—was frantically trying to get the Kulluk out of Alaska waters to avoid paying a $7 million state tax that would have been assessed on January 1, the next day.

For years, the big oil companies had lobbied to open up the Arctic Ocean to drilling; Shell had spent an estimated $5 billion on technology, and, of course, lobbying, to win the rights to drill in the Beaufort Sea. These remote waters north of Alaska are known for polar bears, bowhead whales, and other rare mammals, but also for cruel subzero temperatures, shifting ice floes, hurricane-force winds, and massive waves. Big Oil companies look at this area with dollar signs in their eyes. It is home to as much as one-fifth of the world's remaining oil reserves. But environmentalists—mindful of the ecological harm wreaked by the 1989 *Exxon Valdez* shipwreck—lobbied for years to block Shell from drilling in these more dangerous and more sensitive waters, an effort that was eventually unsuccessful.

No wonder. When Shell did finally launch its Arctic drilling efforts in the fall of 2012, it was such an unmitigated disaster that even the conservative British newspaper *The Telegraph* called it "a comedy caper," asking: "What next? A polar bear attack?" Thwarted by ice, conflicts with the whaling season, a minor fuel spill from the ship intended to help prevent spills, problems with the containment dome meant to prevent another Deepwater Horizon–sized catastrophe, and other foibles, the only thing Shell didn't do that Arctic autumn was produce any oil. The embarrassing grounding of the Kulluk was what you could call the icing on all of this. Shell didn't even attempt to drill in the Arctic waters in 2013. But the dream of tapping massive offshore deposits in risky ventures using untested and unproven technology is still very much alive.

Remember all of the mistakes that we witnessed in the Deepwater Horizon disaster—the failure to have proper containment equipment on hand, the relentless pressure to cut safety corners, the extreme difficulty in capping a massive leak one mile under the surface? Apparently Big Oil, government regulators, and Congress didn't remember a thing, because, amazingly, Washington enacted no new safety legislation in response to the worst oil spill in American history. Deepwater drilling permits were suspended in the Gulf in 2010...for five months, and then they resumed with a vengeance. In 2013, a record number of offshore drilling permits for the Gulf were issued by the feds, and the number of rigs in operation hit a four-year high. After documenting the tragic aftermath of the BP spill for three-plus years, I live in constant fear of what a second accident of that magnitude would do to the still-recovering Gulf.

TAR SANDS

One day in 2008, a flock of 500 ducks landed on a lake in northern Alberta and died almost instantly. Clearly, this was no ordinary lake. Indeed, it was one of the region's toxic tailings lakes—a holding pit for millions of gallons of poisonous residue that are created by the dramatic increase in mining of the Canadian tar sands, now a major source of fuel for North America and for export around the world. The toxic lakes are surrounded by noisemaking cannons that are supposed to scare off migrating ducks and other birds. But on this day the cannons were turned off, for some unknown reason. The company, Syncrude, was fined $3 million for the duck slaughter, but two years later it happened again, killing 550 waterfowl, and then, incredibly, there was another episode in 2010 in which 230 oiled, poisoned birds were euthanized.

That might be the most disgusting environmental impact from Canada's tar sands oil production, but it's far from the only negative effect. If North Americans are addicted to oil, the tar sands fuel is the crack cocaine. It's a heavy, viscous fuel—known as bitumen—that's found trapped in loose sand or in sandstone. Most of the world's deposits—70 percent according to some estimates—are located in western Canada, the third-largest oil deposit of any kind in the world. Like most unconventional oil, it was once thought mostly impractical to develop, before fuel prices soared and extraction technology improved. Now, Big Oil firms from the United States and elsewhere have invested billions of dollars to get it out of the ground.

But the consequences are huge. The heavier fuels made from tar sands are also dirty fuels that create more conventional air pollution and do more than conventional fuels to create the greenhouse gases behind climate change. According to one estimate, a fuel-economical Honda Accord running on a gallon of oil from the tar sands has the same negative effect on global warming as a gas-guzzling Chevy Suburban SUV. One reason for that is that the bitumen has to be extracted by making it more viscous. The methods to do that, such as injecting hot air, steam, or solvents into the sand, burn up a lot of energy. So you're expending massive amounts of energy to get new energy, and you're tearing apart the magnificent Canadian wilderness in the process. To return to my earlier analogy, that's crack addiction thinking, pure and simple.

In the fall of 2013, it became known that a massive tar sands processing facility in Alberta with the soothing-sounding name of Primrose East had been leaking raw bitumen into an adjacent 131-acre lake for months—and the plant's owners were completely baffled in trying to locate the source. Finally, Canadian authorities ordered the operators to drain the entire lake in order to solve the problem. They ought to keep it dry and erect a giant monument there to the folly of the tar sands—but in reality, the black gold rush may continue for years to come.

TRANSPORTATION

There's another downside to the surge in domestic oil and gas production; simply put, all that crude oil or natural gas needs to get
somewhere—to a refinery or, increasingly, to a port for shipment to
emerging markets like China. The drilling boom since the late 2000s
has exposed massive flaws in America's energy infrastructure—and
thus created a whole new category of environmental and public-
health nightmares.

The new crisis was really driven home by two separate incidents
that occurred in 2013. In the small town of Mayflower, Arkansas,
residents woke up on March 29, 2013, to a shock: rivers of thick
black crude oil flowing down their suburban cul-de-sac, cutting
across their freshly mowed lawns, and pouring into storm drains
that empty into a local environmental treasure called Lake Conway.
Most of the bewildered Arkansans didn't even know of the existence
of ExxonMobil's aging, maintenance-challenged Pegasus pipeline,
which was carrying thick oil from the Canadian tar sands through
the woods behind their homes. Now, they were exposed to the same
pathologies of Big Oil that folks along the Gulf Coast had experienced three years earlier with BP.

The oil arrived with the same initial misinformation about the size
of the spill—now estimated to have been at least 235,000 gallons,
maybe more; the same restrictions on flying over the scene of the
spill—which seemed to serve no purpose other than helping the PR
efforts of ExxonMobil; the same denials that an ecologically sensitive body of water, Lake Conway, had been scarred by the spill, even
after independent testing found the presence of hydrocarbons there;
and, worst of all, the same depressing health reports that began to
emerge—probably because of exposure to airborne toxins such as
benzene. Residents of Mayflower soon complained of dizziness,
headaches, nausea, and shortness of breath.

"My headaches were so bad that I was crying," fifty-four-year-old Ann Jarrell, who lives about three-and-a-half football fields from the ExxonMobil spill, told *Inside Climate News*. But she said whenever she left Mayflower on a business trip, her symptoms started to improve. Meanwhile, the Mayflower spill reminded the public of how federal regulators are completely outgunned. In 2010 it was revealed that the U.S. Pipeline Hazardous Materials Administration had just 110 inspectors on its payroll to cover 2.5 million miles of pipeline.

The inability of North America's pipeline infrastructure to keep pace with the energy production boom—both in capacity and safety—meant a dramatic increase in the amount of crude oil and liquefied natural gas now shipped across the continent by rail. But here, the problems with outdated equipment, inadequately trained personnel, and lack of regulation were arguably even more dramatic. Those chickens finally came home to roost in a small, isolated town in rural Quebec called Lac-Megantic.

On July 6, 2013, a train carrying seventy-four tanker cars loaded with oil from North Dakota's Bakken field, the epicenter of the fracking-for-oil boom in the United States, was bound for a refinery in the Canadian province of New Brunswick when the engineer—the only crew member—parked the train for the night several miles west of Lac-Megantic. The understaffed railroad simply left the oil train running, parked on a slight incline. But there were a cascading series of failures, including a fire in the locomotive, which may have deactivated some of the brakes. Just before midnight, the unmanned oil train started hurtling downhill toward the town, where a disco was packed with customers, whipping around sharp curves at 60 mph before its inevitable derailment.

"It was a black blob that came out of nowhere," reported a witness, sixty-five-year-old Gilles Fluet. "I realized they were oil tankers and they were going to blow up, so I yelled that to my friends and

I got out of there. If we had stayed where we were, we would have been roasted." Many were not so lucky. The heat from the massive fireball of the derailment could be felt by people more than a mile away. Authorities eventually concluded that forty-seven people had perished—even though five bodies were never found. It is believed they were completely vaporized.

Rail shipments of crude oil jumped by about 250,000 barrels a day in 2012—the last year for which records are available—and while there is little state regulatory power over cross-country shipments, the feds also seem overmatched in this era of government belt-tightening. The irony is that advocates for new oil pipelines seized on the tragedy at Lac-Megantic and presumably hoped the public would forget the ugly pipeline spill in Arkansas just a few months earlier. Are pipelines or tanker cars safer? The reality is neither. Oil is only 100 percent safe when it's undisturbed, far below the earth.

FRACKING OVER AMERICA

But perhaps the biggest disruption from extreme oil here on U.S. soil has come from the process of fracking.

In the summer of 2011, I was contacted by a couple from rural West Virginia, Dusty and Tamera Hagy. They had found my name by reading some of my environmental online postings, because they were in desperate need of a lawyer with experience and the financial wherewithal to fight big oil companies. I had been following the rise of hydraulic fracturing, or fracking, for natural gas and oil in deep shale formations for a couple of years. But taking on the Hagy case—with the help of a West Virginia-licensed lawyer named Kevin Thompson, with whom I've worked since the Grefer case—opened my eyes to the human cost of fracking.

The Hagys had bought a hilly, eighty-one-acre spread in Jackson County in 1989, but it wasn't until 2007 when a man from Equitable Production Co. showed up to announce that someone else owned the mineral rights and that four wells would be drilled up the hill from their home. It was a fracking nightmare from day one. A worker admitted on tape there had been problems with cement casings in one of the wells; soon, an impoundment pond overflowed, the Hagys' natural pond turned green, and oil slicks appeared in a creek.

Things got worse when natural gas production began in 2008. Around the same time, the Hagy family began to experience unusual health symptoms. Dusty and Tamera began to get headaches and felt tired, as if hung over. Their son visited a doctor in Ohio after experiencing nausea and coughing up blood and developing acid reflux. The doctor told the son to stop drinking the family's well water, and he got better. After Tamera Hagy developed skin rashes, the family had their water tested. It had been examined and found clean before the fracking, but now there were elevated levels of arsenic, lead, and chemicals found in fracking wastewater, and a sharp rise in radon. In January 2009, the Hagys moved out of the house for good.

As they tried to get their life back together, the Hagys even recorded a conversation with an Equitable official in which he admitted that the firm's drilling was responsible for the water contamination. Yet getting justice for the Hagys has so far proved difficult, if not impossible. Other than this worker, Equitable never admitted it was responsible. When the man from Equitable came to their house in 2007, he asked the couple to sign papers that, unbeknownst to the Hagys, held the drillers harmless from most damage. Although we had sunk considerable costs in testing and investigating the Hagys' claims—something most plaintiffs can't afford—the case was thrown out by a lower court judge and his ruling has so far been upheld in appeal. At the end of 2013, we weighed an appeal all the way to the U.S. Supreme Court.

I'm very concerned about the toll that fracking is taking on people like my clients the Hagys, and on the rural way of life in America. It's hard to believe that just a decade ago, only a few engineers and technical people had even heard of fracking, the process of forcing water at high pressure through underground shale rock to extract the many tiny pockets of oil and natural gas that are trapped inside.

A perfect storm in the first decade of the 2000s created this new American gold rush. The fracking process was largely perfected by the oil-services giant Halliburton. In 2005, Halliburton's former CEO, then–Vice President Dick Cheney, helped draft and push an energy bill through the then-GOP-dominated Congress that set the stage for a surge in fracking by barring the EPA from regulating the process under the Safe Water Drinking Act. That meant that Big Gas companies would be able to inject billions of gallons of polluted water into deep wells with little or no oversight.

The result has been an ecological disaster of epic proportions. Remember where my journey as an environmental lawyer started—in the deep woods of Mississippi, fighting Chevron and trying to educate a jury of our peers about the inherent dangers of pulling up so much radioactivity from under the ground and handling it so recklessly. Now, compared to the massive fracking activity taking place, the scale that piled up in Winston Street's rattling yard—dangerous as it was—felt like the proverbial drop in the bucket.

In October 2013, Duke University researchers published one of the most significant reports to date on the radioactivity of fracking wastewater, and the findings were astounding. Fracking companies had been taking the so-called flowback—the water that surges back up to the surface—and shipping it to a local sewage treatment plant in west-central Pennsylvania. The study found that radium levels downstream from that plant were 200 times higher than the levels upstream—so high that only a licensed radioactive disposal facility would be qualified to accept the waste. And this is just one of numerous locations in Pennsylvania where fracking wastewater is routinely dumped in rivers and streams—places where regular folks fish and swim and frequently get their tap water. The fracking industry actually "produces" more of this tainted water than hydrocarbons, although the exact amount is not known.

The same week as the Duke report, a second study by the group Environment America claimed that fracking has produced an astounding 280 billion gallons of toxic tainted water since the Cheney-backed fracking bill passed Congress in 2005—enough to cover Washington, D.C., in a radioactive lagoon twenty-two feet deep! The greatest use and abuse of water resources during the fracking era has taken place in the state of Texas, which during those same years has suffered from extreme drought, pushing humans, livestock, and wildlife to the brink. Concluded the report: "Our analysis shows that damage from fracking is widespread and occurs on a scale unimagined just a few years ago."

Indeed, the damage caused to the U.S. environment by fracking is so extensive that it really deserves a book of its own. Just a few highlights: Scientists are increasingly convinced that deepwell injection of fracking wastes is responsible for swarms of small- to medium-sized earthquakes, often in regions that previously had not experienced much seismic activity. The federal EPA estimates that more than 100,000 tons of toxic air pollutants, including the carcinogen benzene, are released into the atmosphere from fracking activities every year. Families' tap water or their rural wells have been contaminated by methane and other pollutants, most likely the result of shoddy fracking-well casings.

All of this is justified by fracking proponents who note, correctly, that the natural gas produced by fracking is a much cleaner way to run vehicles and operate power plants than the incumbent fuels, such as gasoline made from crude oil, or electric power from coal. And, if you've ever sat in traffic behind a natural gas powered bus, and you remember those black smoke and soot-spewing diesel models of yesteryear, then you'd have to agree that on the surface this is certainly true. But after a decade of fracking, it seems increasingly clear that the risks to the environment simply aren't worth the gains touted by advocates.

The clincher is climate change. At a time when the fate of the planet may well depend on our ability to reduce our emissions of greenhouse gases, almost all of these forms of unconventional "extreme energy" are making the climate problem worse. This manifests itself in many ways—from the billions of dollars spent on deep-sea drilling, even in difficult regions like the Arctic Sea, that strengthen our addictive bond with fossil fuels, to the brutal, energy-intensive extraction of the dirty Canadian tar sands oil. Increasingly, scientists are learning that even fracking does more harm than good when it comes to global warming.

That's because the natural gas that's trapped inside those shale beds is largely methane. The Intergovernmental Panel on Climate Change (IPCC) found that methane traps heat—and presumably warms the planet—at a rate thirty-four times greater than carbon dioxide, which has been the prime focus of the global warming fight. Although the IPCC report said well-maintained wells don't necessarily leak much methane, other surveys have suggested that some fracking wells leak at a rate of 6 to 12 percent, emitting greenhouse gases at a devastating rate.

I was born below sea level. The *least* dire prediction about climate change is that sea levels in the New Orleans area will rise by a foot over the next 100 years; more realistic expectations released a couple of years ago by the Natural Resources Defense Council are that waters will surge and wetlands will subside by a combined total of 4.6 feet, which would make what's left of my beloved Crescent City an island surrounded by the Gulf of Mexico. And the next Hurricane Katrina—and there will be a next one—could sound the death knell for New Orleans.

"GIVING A DAMN" ABOUT THE PLANET

I've tried to show in this book how the tort lawyer is not only the last line of defense for everyday citizens, but also too often the only hope for justice in an otherwise rigged system. Sure, we're a fraternity of high-flying massive egos—swashbuckling on our best days, arrogant on our worst. Some people think that trial lawyers are big jerks. But if that's true on some days, we are always jerks for the people, getting in the face of the faceless corporations. I love what I do, my clients love what I do for them, and the rich guys up in the executive suite can't stand me. They tried to shut me down in Mississippi, and in more recent years they've tried to shut me down in Louisiana. They've tried this through a big-business-backed push to re-brand our efforts to protect the rights of property owners who've been dumped on by Big Oil as "legacy lawsuits" that will be much harder to get before a judge and jury. But they'll never shut down me or my peers completely. Every day, unfortunately, there are Americans who are wronged by a big powerful corporation, and there will always be some battle to fight somewhere.

But while I've been able to win what I call crude justice for lots of regular folks, for pipe-cleaners and refinery workers, for rural landowners and their children, there is one battle that I cannot win in a courtroom—one that is too big for any one trial lawyer to win.

That is the fight to save the Earth from its ruination by fossil fuels.

That struggle is going to require all of us.

It's going to take bold political leaders, ethical business executives, and an engaged, activist citizenry.

It's going to take an effort to make sure that the proposed Keystone XL pipeline—which would increase the environmentally ruinous mining of the Canadian oil sands—is never completed. The plan for a thirty-six-inch pipeline to carry the heavy, toxic crude across sensitive lands in the Great Plains of north-central America (along with a southern section stretching to the Gulf Coast, where the fuel could be refined and shipped overseas) is very much up in the air as I write this; even if President Obama pacifies Big Oil and tentatively approves the Keystone XL in 2014, environmentalists will, and should, fight to ensure it's never built.

Why? For one thing, a spill of thick, toxic tar sands oil—not a hard thing to imagine, given America's dismal recent record with pipeline safety—into the Ogallala aquifer would poison the fresh drinking water supply for a couple of million people in and around Nebraska. And the greater danger is the seemingly more abstract one: Saying "yes" to the pipeline and giving tacit approval for the exploitation of the dirty tar sands in Alberta would send the signal that America is simply not serious about fighting global warming. The renowned climate scientist James Hansen said that signing off on the carbon-intensive energy plan means "either that governments don't understand the situation or that they just don't give a damn."

It's time to start giving a damn.

It's going to take the new evidence of widespread radioactive contamination from fracking to inspire a renewed effort to do what we failed to do right the first time, twenty years ago: to create a regulatory framework that will stop the widespread dumping of radioactive oil wastes, especially the billions of gallons of polluted water from fracking. It's time to dispose of radioactive wastes in an approved facility, and to undo the regulations that Dick Cheney and his cronies imposed in America that have allowed frackers to pollute our waterways at will.

Most importantly, it's time to make good on our pledge to make safe, clean renewable forms of energy the centerpiece of America's energy policy. In 2000, Germany looked at the future of power generation, and the threat of global warming, and enacted a measure called the Renewable Energies Act, the opening salvo in a revolution that the Germans called "die Energiewende." The almost comical irony is that what the Germans were doing was remarkably similar to the energy policy that President Jimmy Carter had proposed for America in the late 1970s—but had been reversed by a generation of Big Oil hegemony and climate science denialism.

For nearly a generation, German policy has focused on increasing the market share of wind, solar, and biomass energy from burning renewable materials such as wood, and the payoff has been enormous. Germany has increased the energy market share of renewables from 6.3 percent in 2000 to more than 20 percent today, and you have to think its ambitious goal of 80 percent by 2050 is doable. Germany has lowered the price that companies pay for electricity, and it has created as many as 180,000 new jobs making things like solar panels and wind rotors.

If that sounds familiar, it is essentially the energy program that President Obama promised Americans in 2008, and that he has been largely blocked from delivering by a faction that calls itself the Tea Party but might as well be called the Oil Party. By the start of the second term, the Obama administration was still talking about additional funding and loan guarantees for innovative green energy initiatives—the push that should have begun a generation ago. It's getting late—late for America, late for the planet. But it's not too late.

It's easy for folks to feel powerless when confronting the billion-dollar bank books of Big Oil. But one thing I've learned from my recent experience with the Deepwater Horizon debacle: Everyday people can make a difference. Over the last several years, I've worked with regular Joes and Janes like a small-plane pilot, a scuba diver, chemists, and other crusading activists to undo the narrative spun by not only one of the world's largest oil companies, BP, but by weak-kneed parts of the federal government. And we've been winning that PR war. There are countless others fighting Big Oil and Gas in their own hometowns—who take on the frackers at rural town hall meetings, or who stage noisy protests against the Keystone XL. I urge you to join them.

The oil companies have tried to shut me down for twenty years, and they've failed. But you can put me out of business—at least my current calling of suing the likes of Chevron, ExxonMobil, and BP. Get involved where you live and in local elections and conserve energy where you can. Help put our great nation into oil-addiction rehab. If I never sued an oil company again—never got a single new client whose bones ached or whose lungs burned from working in radioactive dust or breathing in an oil slick—I'd be a happy lawyer indeed. I'd surely find other cases to work on, or maybe I'll just set sail for the South Pacific—with the peace of mind of knowing that New Orleans won't be under four feet of water when I get home.

Betting big—and winning jackpots for my clients—has been the thrill of a lifetime. But we can't roll the dice on Planet Earth.

ACKNOWLEDGMENTS

WHEN I DECIDED about seven years ago that I wanted to tell my story, I knew that it would not be an easy task. I was right. But I was also lucky. I had a lot of help from a lot of good people, and I want to write a short note of profound thanks—with apologies in advance if I missed anybody.

First of all, I wanted to say thanks to so many friends and clients from over the years who were willing to take a few minutes out, in person or over the phone, to share their own memories and impressions of the things that have happened in my career...so far. I am truly grateful to Mike Stag, Ron Austin, Winston Street, Clark Street, Bonny Schumaker, Marylee Orr, Marco Kaltofen, Al Walker, Richard Brackin, John Volpe, Paul Templet, Eddie Fuente, Stan Waligora, and all the others who gave the most valuable gift of all: their time. I also want to thank Jason Tullos at my law firm SmithStag LLC for critical help with the research. Many thanks also go out to my dear friends Curtis Robinson and Peter Wendel, whose advice and assistance in the early stages of the book were critical to its completion.

Even with all their help, it took several strokes of good fortune to make *Crude Justice* a reality. I owe a lot to my good friend David

Brock for connecting me with a literary agent, Will Lippincott of Lippincott Massie McQuilkin. Both Will and his colleague Jason Anthony played a critical role in making this project happen and in putting out the more-than-occasional fire. They also connected me with a writer, Will Bunch, who worked closely with me in crafting the tome you are now holding.

Will L. and Jason also connected me with a publisher who truly shared my vision for this project: BenBella Books. All the people at BenBella—but especially Glenn Yeffeth, Erin Kelley, Adrienne Lang, and Jessika Rieck—were patient and incredibly helpful in guiding a first-time author through the long journey from a rough idea to a finished manuscript.

The lawyers who helped and influenced me throughout my career deserve a lot of credit for my success. I want to particularly thank my mentor and friend Jack Harang. Despite the many bumps in the long road of our relationship, I will always care deeply for him. He is still the best trial lawyer I know.

Finally, I want to thank my mother, Judy, for working so hard in order for me to be the person I am and Barry for sticking with me all these years.

INDEX